THE
LUKE
PROJECT

THE LUKE PROJECT

PROJECT

*What
My Son's Life
and Death
is Teaching Me*

CAROLYN
VAN DER VORST

ISBN (paperback): 979-8-218-71998-2

———————

Edited & designed by Kairos Book Design & Editing
kairosbookdesign.com

Editor: Rachel Weisbrot
Designer: Benita Thompson

~ for my son, Luke,
whose life and death are expanding my heart, mind, and soul

~ for Dirk, Hannah, Jesse, and Lydia,
who have held my heart together through it all

~ for everyone on the journey of recovery from loss and trauma

TABLE OF CONTENTS

PREFACE

Why I'm Writing this Book

1. **Writing gives me joy.** As a way to start taking gradual steps out of the darkness and chaos immediately after Luke's passing, I was encouraged to commit to doing at least one thing a day that gave me joy. So I took a lot of walks outside in nature. I went swimming. I did yoga. I got a new puppy.

   I've since learned that doing what gives you joy just might be the most important thing you can do in your life. Following your joy leads you to your purpose. It helps you live your most authentic self. I find joy in expressing myself through the written word. I appreciate the time and space the written word allows me to communicate thoughtfully. And what I most want to communicate are words of love and truth. I hope my words might move, inspire, and comfort you. If they do, my joy will be multiplied.

2. **To honor Luke.** Shortly after Luke passed, I began to have a sense that he wanted to partner with me in some sort of ongoing work, that he had messages and wisdom to share. I had no idea what that would look like or how that could be done. During the next couple of years I sought out many types of healing, both traditional (talk therapy, group therapy) and non-traditional (spiritual healers). The sense that Luke and I

still had work to do together grew as various healers, un-prompted, told me the same.

In January of 2023 I was practising yoga, bending over for a pose, when out of the blue I received the words: "The Luke Project." I had no idea what "The Luke Project" was but I had an inner knowing that it was something Luke wanted to do with me. So I took note of it and tucked that experience away, trusting that the meaning would eventually be revealed.

In May of 2024 I was reading Sarina Baptista's book, *My View from Heaven*. In it her son in spirit, J.T., explains that when our souls sign up for another life, each life is referred to as a "project." The idea is that in each life we intend to learn something and/or help someone else learn something. Each life is a learning assignment we give ourselves for the purpose of mutual expansion. Ah— "The Luke Project"! It made sense to me now. A book about Luke's life, and my life, the intertwining of our lives, and what we're learning through it all.

3. **For personal and mutual healing and expansion.** Several years ago in Celebrate Recovery, I learned that, "You can't heal what you don't reveal." Sharing our struggles, talking about our pain, is healing in itself. Just verbalizing it or journaling about it, putting it out there, outside of ourselves, somehow neutralizes the experience. This is an innate knowing we have inside ourselves and it's what keeps therapists and confessional-booth priests employed. On the other hand, what we bury festers. The "dark" secrets we keep to ourselves, too ashamed to bring them to light, or too scared to face the emotional overload unearthing them might bring—

those buried experiences don't just fade into the night. We carry them in more sinister, unconscious ways like depression, rage, and addiction, which make relationships difficult and keep us from knowing our true selves.

I've come to believe that our entire lives are really a journey of healing. No one escapes this life trauma-free. We all experience hardships and challenges, in a plethora of different ways. Sharing the story of my life with Luke as authentically as I can is a part of my own healing journey. I know that although your pain and challenges may differ from mine, you too are on a healing journey. I hope the story of Luke and me touches and expands your heart and mind, as it is expanding mine, so that we can continue to embrace life and *all* that it holds for us.

INTRO

Ground Zero

Ground Zero, place of nothing, place of mass destruction

Nuclear explosions, towers smashed to the ground, center of intense, violent change.

A terror never known before, everything upended, nothing makes sense in those moments of frenzy—Is This Really Happening?! What Is Happening?!

"Ground yourself" in moments of trauma … where is the ground now? Even it is shaking.

Unmoored, unanchored, a deep knowing that everything has changed, nothing will be the same. That's all we know, all we can know.

A space once full of life, future, hope, now filled with … zero.

Luke's death is my Ground Zero. An unspeakable trauma. The point at which everything changed.

"Hi, my name is Carolyn and my son, Luke, died by suicide on September 17, 2021. He was 19 years old."

The first time I could barely choke out those words. Saying it out loud confirmed the details once again, forcing me to accept the unacceptable. My throat closed up, as if trying to keep the memory of my traumatic loss down and buried. I was tired of crying all the time, sometimes uncontrollably, and I didn't want to start that flood again.

Verbalizing the facts of our child's suicide was the prescribed protocol for beginning our weekly meetings with the Coping After Suicide moms' group I had committed to for ten weeks. I learned about the group through the Heartlight Center, the organization that hosted the space in which we held Luke's memorial open house.

It was January 2022, four months after Luke's death, although time was a somewhat irrelevant concept for me then. In her book, *Wintering: The Power of Rest and Retreat in Difficult Times*, Katherine May describes being "Somewhere Else." She describes how when a tragedy happens, it jerks you out of the mainstream, the normal, the busyness of everyday life into an alternate space, almost an alternate reality. Somewhere Else. That's what the months, even years, after Luke's death felt like for me. Like I was living in a parallel reality. Which was okay. I felt like most of "normal" life didn't apply to me anymore anyway.

Luke died at 7:35am on a Friday morning. About five minutes before, he sent my husband and I a text saying, "I love you." That was weird. That was not a phrase we threw around a lot in our family, and especially not at 7:30am. I responded: "We love you too Luke. Everything okay?" No response.

It so happened that morning I had an early appointment with a family in Golden—a coaching session that would hopefully help the family with their adopted son's challenging behaviors. I had to get on the road to reach their house on time, so I put the text exchange out of my mind and made the drive over. About ten minutes into our session my cell phone rang, or rather vibrated, since I had it on silent. First I ignored it, but it kept ringing so I finally looked at the number. I didn't recognize it so again I ignored it and went on with the session.

Soon my phone rang again. This time it was Luke's girlfriend, K, calling from college in Pennsylvania. This was unusual. A feeling of dread started to build in me. K tearfully told me that she and Luke tracked each other's phones, and she knew where he was. It was a location we were both familiar with. Luke had threatened to kill himself before, at this very spot. I tearfully made a hasty exit from the family's house, them wondering what happened and me unable to tell them, unwilling to give voice to the terrifying possibility. I'll never forget their perplexed and saddened 3-year-old son watching me out the front screen door as I sped off to face the unthinkable.

In true Luke style, he made an Instagram post of his suicide note and photo from the place he jumped. He included a request to his friends to "please make sure his parents see this since they're not on Instagram." By the time I arrived at the scene, my husband, D, was there, as well as what seemed like an overkill of emergency vehicles. D confirmed the awful truth. I asked the police investigator if I could see Luke. The answer was no because this was a crime scene. The yellow tape had already been secured around the area. Law enforcement had to verify that there had been no foul play, that this was indeed a suicide. Besides, I may not want to see Luke's body in the condition it was in. I fell to the curb, all the life drained out of my own body. I started shivering, a visceral reaction to the horror I couldn't see beyond the tape and the structures between us and Luke. A Victim's Advocate put her arm around me and told me that mental health issues are like cancer or any other physical disease—some survive and some don't.

Also at the scene was a couple I had never met (and that kept their distance); they were the parents of one of Luke's friends. Luke called his friend's mom "Mama D." Honestly, I was so pissed to see them there. Couldn't even this moment be ours and ours alone? Did we have to be reminded, even here and now, of Luke's constant search for other caregivers, as if we were never enough? And to see the cops verifying the news for them, and she falling to her knees—what right did they have to know what happened?! Luke wasn't even their son!

We realized then that social media is faster than any pair of human legs. We raced to our youngest daughter's workplace, praying that we could break this to her before she saw it on her phone. Thankfully we made it. Then home to tell our other two children. Reactions were mixed. Sadness and guilt: "I tried so hard!" (to keep Luke here). Anger: "Well, this is the ultimate family sabo-tage!" Body-shaking sobs. Devastation all around. Ground Zero.

LESSON ONE

The Safety Net

I've never walked a tightrope or flown on a trapeze, at least not literally. Figuratively, most of us have. Life tends to give us those experiences that make us wonder if we'll be able to find the next hand hold or maintain our balance or land on our feet. Sometimes there's a lot of uncertainty and the things we trust in to hold us up appear rather tenuous.

It helps a lot to know there's a safety net below. It's there to fall into when we take a misstep or when our apparatus fails us. I've always believed in the existence of the safety net. Some might call it God, or Love, or the Design of the Universe—that underlying force that is ultimately supporting us, that becomes especially evident at the worst of times. Luke's death was my "worst of times". Accordingly, the Safety Net appeared, sometimes seemingly out of thin air, in ways I could not have planned or predicted.

The Preparatory Dream

Several weeks before Luke died, I had a dream. An especially vivid one.

I found myself high up, looking down on a huge, white, feathery bird with its wings outstretched. On its back there was someone laying prostrate, facing up. I imagined what it might feel like to be lying on that bird. It felt like total softness, like infinite feathers or down, yet totally supported. It felt like being totally carried and cared for. The bird was kind of hovering in one spot, much lower than me but at the same level as some flat rooftops of buildings. It was a very vivid, comforting vision that I returned to when I couldn't get to sleep or woke up in the night. I would imagine myself being carried in comfort on those feathers.

About a month after Luke passed away it hit me. When Luke fell to his death he didn't land on the ground. He landed on a flat rooftop. Up until this moment it had merely seemed like a strange (but vivid) detail of my dream: the fact that the big, beautiful, comforting bird was hovering at the level of a flat rooftop. Now my heart and mind immediately made connections. I realized it was Luke's body that I had seen pillowed in the white feathers of that bird. To me the message was: "It's okay, I'm okay, I was taken care of beautifully at the moment of my death. I was supported, I was at peace." It had been gut-wrenchingly horrifying for me to think of Luke, my son, lying there alone in his mangled body, in the pit of despair that incomprehensibly enabled him to deny every human instinct to survive. I wasn't there. I wasn't even allowed to see or hold him at the scene of his death. He died comfortless. And knowing that, I was comfortless.

That dream gave me comfort. The comfort of knowing my son was okay. Even at the moment of his tragic, horrible death, he was okay. He was supported, carried. Was the bird God? Or an angel? To me it doesn't really matter. What I knew then, deep inside me, was that my son was okay—even in the moment of his death, my son was okay. Something greater than his pain, and our pain, was involved: a loving, expansive, eternal Presence that came up under him to support him and was supporting us all. A huge divine safety net. A few months after Luke died, I got a beautiful tattoo symbolizing the bird in my dream, with "LMV" (Luke Moise Van der Vorst) inked on one of the wings. It is a constant, imprinted reminder of this comfort.

The Preparatory Scrapbook

When each of my children graduated from high school I presented them with a scrapbook of their lives. Luke graduated in May of 2020, right in the middle of the Covid-19 pandemic. The school did hold a graduation ceremony of sorts, a month after the school year ended, in the football field with social distancing. Kudos to the school for their efforts, but the sparsely attended ceremony was another reminder of the bleakness of that whole year. Luke and his class missed out on all those senior year celebrations and parties, including prom. Luke's girlfriend's parents and sister made a little prom in their backyard just for Luke and her—a sweet little antidote to the FOMO that was a hallmark of that time.

Back to the scrapbook … honestly, I had struggled with the decision to even make one for Luke. The previous years, before Covid, had felt like hell with him. This was much more than just the terrible teens. There were levels of unresolved emotions and issues that could find no outlet but rage and rejection. Not just for Luke, but for me (more on that later). I wondered if I really wanted to invest all the time and energy into making a scrapbook for him. I didn't even know how I'd fill the book since Luke had basically stopped communicating with us or going with us on family outings—there were years when I had hardly any photos of him. But the Greater Something was urging me to do it. So I pushed aside my frustrations with Luke, the hurt I felt, the anger that I never knew I was capable of feeling and expressing before

11

Luke became my son, and I made the scrapbook. To fill in the empty pages, I reached out to his high school teachers (Luke was a favorite among them) and other important adult people in his life and asked them to write a letter of encouragement and reflection for him. Every person I reached out to provided me with one. At the time, I didn't realize how important making and contributing to that scrapbook would be, for all of us.

We decided to have a small memorial service for Luke with just the family and a few friends and then an open house for anyone who wanted to come. I had the idea to enlarge pages of Luke's scrapbook and display them, along with memorabilia from the activities and times commemorated in those pages. My dear friend, J, drove five hours to be with us and help in any way she could, that first weekend after Luke died. She helped me decide which scrapbook pages to display and drove with me to the copy center. My emotions were still raw. I felt like I was largely going through the motions, not really present but getting things done. I broke down in tears at the counter. The copy center guy, A, might have been an angel in disguise (hmmm, his first name did start with an A!). He went above and beyond with the job, which included memorial photo cards and pocket-sized versions of the Serenity Prayer. He called me with updates and in the end only charged us $170 for what was actually a $900 (yikes!) job. Later I stopped by with a thank you card and a little gift card for him, to express our thanks. I "happened" to catch him as he was leaving the store after his shift, and he gave me a hug and asked how I was doing. In that vulnerable time, that meant so much to me. The support of a stranger.

Who knew that scrapbook would serve to be such a point of connection, not only for Luke and I before he passed (his girlfriend told me he looked at it all the time), but for the 200+ others who came to honor Luke at his memorial? The scrapbook I almost didn't make.

All the People that Held Us

Two weeks after his suicide, our family held a memorial service and open house for Luke. In all the preparations for, and the happenings of the day of the service, that safety net became apparent in so many synchronistic ways! I felt so HELD during that time. Many people came to our home with gifts of comfort: warm blankets, warm soup, gift cards for meals, hand-crocheted prayer shawls for each member of our family (which we all wore for those first weeks/months and I still use regularly—there's nothing like warmth around your shoulders to bring you comfort!), chocolate, flowers, home-made banana bread, and of course many hugs and tears. We received so many beautiful cards which I strung across a wall of our dining room and kept up for the entire year, to remind me of all that support.

The memorial was held on October 2, 2021. Because of the still-present Covid threat, the quickness with which everything transpired, and the distances our family would have to travel (everyone being in Canada), only D's sister and brother-in-law were able to make it to the memorial. We will always be grateful they did. At that time, it was required to take a Covid test and submit it before being allowed to fly across the border. It "so happened" that my supervisor from work (who had just given her two-weeks notice a few days before Luke died) had a neighbor who was the CEO of a Covid-testing company and could expedite the process for my in-laws. It was also difficult and expensive to secure a hotel for them on such short notice, since at the time we didn't have

13

room to host them in our home. During one of the many heart-wrenching calls we made to friends and family to inform them of Luke's death, one friend (whom I hadn't spoken to in probably over a year) mentioned that they had recently renovated their basement, and did we have anyone who needed a place to stay? D's sister and brother-in-law ended up having the Hilton B&B experience at their home, and only a five-minute drive from our house!

Rhonda Roorda is a well-known and well-respected author of several books on transracial adoption. She herself is a transracial adoptee: a black woman adopted into a white family. We first met her in person at African-Caribbean Heritage Camp and discovered that she was not only adopted into a white family, but into a Dutch, Christian Reformed family, like ours! She, D and I were all graduates of Calvin College in Grand Rapids, Michigan. Beyond what Rhonda had written in her books, we were privileged to have had more intimate conversations with her about the challenges of being a transracial family. Amazingly, Rhonda just "happened" to be in Denver the weekend of Luke's memorial and "happened" to get in touch with us. She wasn't able to come to the memorial but came to help us set up the Open house room the day before and then came over for dinner. Everything was happening so fast, and I was exhausted. I had no dinner plans. It was surreal to be sitting around the table with Rhonda Roorda in our home, on the eve of Luke's memorial, processing Luke's death and the challenges of being a transracial adoptee and family. As we—Rhonda, D, myself, my in-laws, and our adult children—were in deep conversation, the doorbell rang. It was our friends who were hosting D's sister and brother-in-law. They were as surprised to see all the people around our table as we were to see them! Fortuitously, they presented us with a huge pan of lasagna, bread, salad and baked goods—enough to feed all eight of us!

The safety net metaphor I'm using here took on flesh the day of Luke's memorial, in the myriad of people who showed up and literally let us fall into their arms. It seemed almost miraculous that so many came (how did they all hear about it?) and from every facet of our lives. There was Mrs. K, Luke's kindergarten teacher. Senseis G and C, Luke's karate teachers who had coached him from white to brown belt status in elementary school. Luke's youth pastor and friends from Colorado Community Church. The pastor and multiple friends from First Christian Reformed Church, the church that financed Luke's adoption back in 2004 and guided him in his faith during his elementary years. Many friends from Luke's recent years working at Starbucks (where he was a star employee). Luke's Starbucks supervisor, C, one of the last people to see Luke alive. Luke's best friends from high school and several teachers who had a special bond with Luke. His best friend from middle school, with his family. My YMCA yoga instructor, S! And G, the founder and director of Resilience Rising, a non-profit for which I had worked for four years, surprised us and flew in from California.

Several of my coworkers not only showed up but brought Chick-fil-A for our family. Luke's girlfriend arranged for Starbucks to provide refreshments, at no charge to us. The family of one of Luke's close friends brought popcorn and licorice, two of Luke's favorite snacks, to put on the tables. At the time, D was working as the Director of Spiritual Care at Denver Health Medical Center. Basically, his whole department was professionally trained in gracefully dealing with suffering and death. One of his chaplains gave the message at Luke's memorial. Another played her harp.

Many other chaplains came to the open house to offer comfort and support. It felt like every supportive community we and Luke had ever been a part of was there, holding us.

The Gift of Butterflies

Just before she came to visit us that first weekend after Luke died, my friend, J, "happened" to have participated in a butterfly release at an event in the mountain town where she lived. When she mentioned that, my heart lifted, thinking of releasing butterflies at Luke's memorial. J found out the particulars of the butterfly-release company and passed the info on to me.

Luke had been privileged to have the same guidance counselor, A, for all four years at his high school. Over that time A had become a safe space for Luke. She understood, more than most, the mental health struggles Luke had been going through. And she happened to live in our neighborhood; in fact, a couple of blocks from our home. That fact may have saved Luke's life one terrible night when he ran from our home in a rage, threatening to kill himself, but found himself, instead, pounding on A's door. A ended up admitting Luke to the Psych ED and called me from there. It was strange and awkward and, for me, shame-inducing to tag-team with A, a school professional I barely knew, in this raw and vulnerable and terrible experience of trying to keep my son alive. However, I never felt judged by A and I knew she cared deeply for my son.

When I asked, A immediately and enthusiastically responded: yes, she would take care of the butterfly release at Luke's memorial. She ordered, paid for and facilitated the whole butterfly release. What a gift. During the Open house about 75 of us gathered in the small garden area by Luke's memorial boulder. There was something tangibly comforting about opening the delicate paper envelope with the butterfly inside, witnessing it wake up in my hands, briefly adjust, and then take a colorful flight to the bounty of flowers all around us. I hoped, and somehow knew, that Luke was experiencing something like that. Waking up and taking flight in a new and beautiful world.

The Memorial Boulder

Luke's boulder … another lesson in miracles. It was not hard to pick the site for Luke's memorial and open house. D was already familiar with it. Horan & McConaty Cremation Gardens was just minutes from our home and a perfect oasis nestled peacefully in the bustle of Denver. I loved the lotus pond, beside which we had Luke's outdoor private memorial service, and the waterfalls, the manicured green spaces, trees, flowers, and magical paths weaving in and out of everything. I knew I needed to be outside, with lots of space and air to breathe, and the sun shining on my face, to get through Luke's memorial service. Indeed, that day turned out to be the perfect day to be outside, a beautiful fall day. Along the paths in the garden were memorial bricks, the size typically used in construction on, say, a brick house. Originally, we were thinking of buying one of those for Luke. The cost was several hundred dollars. Our daughter, L, had the idea of starting a Go-FundMe to give people the opportunity to contribute. And they did! The money kept pouring in, exceeding our wildest expectations. In the end we received over $8000! Enough to buy a boulder in a special part of the garden to memorialize Luke. How fitting for a young man who spent his final days in the town of Boulder and loved to both climb and boulder. Fitting, too, for Luke to be memorialized on something rough and unpolished, with jagged edges, like the life he lived.

The Videographer Who Got Us

The safety net and the providential synchronicities continued to materialize on the day of Luke's memorial. Everything felt like a divine set-up, like everything concerning memorializing Luke had somehow been prepared for us beforehand. This became evident again in the person who video recorded and live-streamed Luke's service. Horan & McConaty recommended and arranged for a company called BXcited to help us out. Turns out BXcited was a young black man, S. Just seeing him there gave me comfort. It felt like the universe was honoring Luke, even in this. After the service we were given a gift bag. Inside were five T-shirts, one for each of our family (I remember feeling like we were one T-shirt short), each with "You Are Worth It" stenciled in embossed letters. Turns out S's sister had died by suicide a couple of years earlier. He made these T-shirts and sold them to honor his sister and support suicide prevention. He got what we were going through. We felt like he went the extra mile to capture not only the essence of Luke's memorial service, but the essence of who Luke was as a person, by slowly filming the scrapbook pages and memorabilia display we had set up at the open house. I've worn holes in my "You Are Worth It" T-shirt, I wear it so much.

The Preparatory Job

About a year and a half before Luke died, I secured a job training adoptive and foster families in trauma-informed caregiving. The assumption is (and correctly so, I believe) that all adopted and foster children have experienced trauma. Sometimes I felt like a bit of a sham teaching and training others while I was keenly aware of my many short-comings in parenting my own traumatized child. On the other hand, I could deeply empathize with the challenges these parents and caregivers were experiencing, and my heart went out to both them and their children.

Looking back, my work helped prepare me for Luke's death in the way that it helped me to make sense of things. D and I were so naive when we embarked on the adoption journey. The idea that all adopted children are traumatized children was so far from our brains. We were just happy and excited to welcome this child into our lives and home! We had no idea of the many ways Luke's trauma would play out in our family: from life-long issues with food and eating, to a pattern of self-sabotage, to resisting attachment, to explosive anger, etc. The training and work I did in trauma-informed care helped me understand Luke's trauma at a level I had not before. That understanding helped move me from resentment and anger to empathy and even admiration for the incredible challenges Luke faced in his life as an adoptee (never mind the added layers of being a transracial adoptee and living as a young black man in the USA). When Luke died, I didn't have big "why" questions, like many do in the case of suicide. A friend of mine recently said that when he thinks of people who die by suicide, he thinks of people who need rest. Yes, Luke needed rest.

A little side note: The administrative staff person who set me up with a work computer, the first person I met at this job, was Haitian and her surname was Pierre-Louise. Luke's birth surname is Pierre and our Haitian daughter, L's, birth surname is Louise. At the time, the coincidence made me wonder. The staff person and I had a little conversation and laughed about it. Now, I believe that "coincidence" was a sign of the impact that learning about trauma-informed care would have, not only on my clients but also on my family and on me.

Maybe you recall from the introduction that I was at a client's home the morning Luke died. I was coaching this biracial family through the difficult behaviors of their adopted 4-year-old African-American son. Needless to say, I felt a deep connection with this family. I also felt terrible to have left that morning the way I did, suddenly, with no explanation and tears streaming down my face. Well, this family surprised me and came to Luke's memorial open house (again, I don't know how they found out about it) with their two little boys. The boys ate popcorn, drew and wrote on our memorial leaf tree, and released butterflies from their small hands. It warmed and melted my heart to see them there, participating in our grief. Turns out this family is no stranger to grief—another of their sons had been born still, years earlier. We bonded over the loss of our sons. They were an incredible, and unexpected, source of support to me during those early months of grief.

The Preparatory Therapist

Several months before Luke's passing I started seeing a new therapist, R. I was experiencing angst about my career path. I enjoyed the work I was doing but felt there was more or something different that I was missing. R specialized in working with women and incorporated spirituality into her counseling. Her practice is called "Live Your Knowing," a title that really resonated with me. It wasn't until I was faced with my own grief that I realized that another of R's specialties was grief counseling! I met with R weekly for a year and a half after Luke's passing. The 30-minute bike ride to and from her office was in itself healing for me; it gave me the regular opportunity to do something physical and be out in nature. Again, I felt like R was part of that safety net that had been divinely spread for me, without my awareness, just a few months earlier, in anticipation of Luke's passing.

Supported

Supported, supported, supported. Like resting on the strong, stable, pillowy support of the large white bird in my dream—that's what I remember most of the days and months following Luke's death. I was lost, disoriented, despairing ... and supported. Amazingly supported, miraculously supported, in ways I did not expect. I believe that's how it was for Luke at the moment he left his body, and I was blessed to experience just a fraction of that.

LESSON TWO

There Are Wonders and Signs All Around

It was wonderful and awful
An awful, wonderful time
A wonderful, awful time
Awe-full—when you peel away the shock, the horror, the despair, the
total derailment, can the awful be filled with awe?

Wonders

It's a wonder that Luke survived even his first two years.

Moise Pierre (Luke) was born in Port-au-Prince, Haiti on February 23, 2002. His mother, Ismane Pierre, was 20 years old, homeless, and jobless. Four years earlier (as she told us when we met her) she had become pregnant with Luke's brother and was consequently kicked out of her parents' home. When she became pregnant with Luke, Luke's birth father left her. I can only imagine the desperation and fear that drove Ismane to finally bring Luke to Hopital Espoir when he was 9 months of age and only weighed a little over 10 pounds. (What depths of resilience enable a baby to survive all those months of malnourishment?!)

Hopital Espoir is part of The Foundation for the Children of Haiti, run by Gladys Sylvestre, a woman driven by her faith in God, her love for the children of her country, and her generous heart. Gladys told us that they weren't sure Moise Pierre would survive—he was so severely malnourished when he came to the hospital. But after some months, with much emotional and physical nurturing from hospital staff, Luke did indeed survive and, understandably, became a favorite of his caregivers. Of course, he was also extraordinarily cute which naturally endeared him to anyone he met.

While Luke Moise was recovering at the hospital, his birth mother was coming to what must have been the agonizing realization that she did not have the resources to take care of him. She relinquished him to the care of the Rainbow of Love orphanage, also a part of The Foundation for the Children of Haiti. After regaining his physical strength, Luke Moise transitioned from the hospital to the orphanage. He would live there for the next year—learning his first words, taking his first steps, and creating his first bonds with his multiple caregivers.

It's a wonder that we were able to bring Luke out of Haiti at the time we did.

Haiti ("Ayiti") means "land of high mountains" in the indigenous Taino-Arawak language, and refers to the mountains on the western side of the country. Perhaps the most famous Haitian proverb—"Beyond mountains there are mountains"—speaks not only to the topography of this tiny island nation but to the continual struggles Haiti has had to overcome throughout its remarkable history. Haiti is the only country in the western hemisphere in which slaves were able to successfully revolt (against French rule) and establish an independent country (in 1804). Unfortunately, since then, the country has been a political and economic pawn of both external international powers and internal corrupt leadership. Add to that the seemingly constant barrage of natural disasters that buffet Haiti—Category 5 hurricanes and Magnitude 7.2 earthquakes—and you have a nation experiencing almost constant turmoil and upheaval.

Little did we know that our experience with Luke would largely reflect the pool of energy he came from. Turmoil, upheaval, struggle, uncertainty—we experienced all of that with Luke, starting with the adoption process.

On August 20, 2001, I mailed our formal adoption application to Dillon International, the state-side agency that coordinated adoptions with The Foundation for the Children of Haiti. It would take over a year and a half to finally be matched with Moise Pierre and then almost another year to welcome him into our home. The length of three pregnancies plus.

Finally, in November of 2003, we received word that we could come to Haiti and pick up our son. We bought our plane tickets, my dad and step-mom drove from Canada to take care of our three other children, and we made arrangements to stay with missionary friends in Haiti during our stay. A couple of days before we were to board our plane, we were strongly advised to cancel our trip because the American immigration office in Haiti had a new requirement: Luke's birth mother had to undergo a DNA test to prove that she was really his birth mother and therefore had the right to relinquish him. This requirement came as a complete surprise to Gladys—she had never before, in all her 20 years of facilitating adoptions, been required to do this. Once again, an unexpected delay and disappointment. However, our family had the unexpected joy of celebrating American Thanksgiving at home with our Canadian grandparents, and we were especially thankful that they could and did commit to taking care of our kids again, whenever the doors should open for us to go to Haiti.

The required DNA test was completed in January 2004.

February 7, 2004 — My dad and step-mom (Oma and Opa, as our family endearingly referred to them) arrived, once again, to take care of Luke's three older siblings while D and I traveled to Haiti.

February 9 — We arrived in Port-au-Prince.

(February 5) — *Just a few days before we arrived, on February 5, armed militants had taken over the city of Gonaives, just 88 miles north of Port-au-Prince. The Associated Press reported that thousands of protestors were yelling, "Aristide must go!" and "The revolution has begun!" Neighboring Dominican Republic had ordered its military to tighten security along the border. The coup to oust President Jean-Bertrand Aristide had begun.*

February 10 — We met Luke Moise for the first time. We were thrilled to finally see him! He was not happy to see us. I remember all the other children were running wild circles around us calling out "mama!" and "papa!" while Luke took shelter in the laps and arms of his nannies. We were able to hold him a little and observe him a lot during that first visit. It felt surreal, and honestly, sad. We were ripping this little boy away from everything he knew, everything familiar and comforting to him, and somehow he seemed to know that.

February 13 — *The political violence and demonstrations had spread to the streets of Port-au-Prince. Again from the Associated Press, "American aid workers and missionaries fled Haiti's mounting crisis Friday as a new round of violence broke out in the capital. Gangs in the city fired shots and hurled rocks at anti-government protesters, injuring at least 20."*

February 13 was my birthday, and the year I turned 37. That day I was given the gift of meeting Luke Moise's birth mother, Ismane. She was very thin and small—we looked like big, white, Dutch giants beside her! She seemed embarrassed and uncomfortable to be with us and didn't make much eye contact at all. However, we did see her flash her big, beautiful smile, her pearly-white teeth perfectly positioned—exactly the smile Luke would grow into and use to charm and disarm many an unsuspecting female! When we asked how she picked the name "Moise" she told us that the lady she was working as a maid for at the time suggested it. "Moise" is French for Moses, the name the princess of Egypt gave her adopted Hebrew child, according to the Biblical story. For Luke Moise, his name would become his destiny.

February 15 — *The Associated Press reports that "more than 1000 protestors defy government loyalists and take to the streets in Port-au-Prince, Haiti, to demonstrate against President Jean-Bertrand Aristide."*

February 17 — Needless to say, being out on the streets in Port-au-Prince at this time was a risky endeavor. However, we had our appointment with the USA Immigration and Naturalization Service (INS) in downtown Port-au-Prince on February 17. Without the documents they would provide us, we would not be legally able to take Luke out of Haiti and into the US. My husband, D, is a brave man, not easily intimidated by danger or challenge, so we hopped into our missionary friends' jeep with him at the wheel and made the harrowing drive into downtown Port-au-Prince. Providentially, we did not run into much mayhem, besides a burning tire or two in the streets which we easily avoided. After waiting a couple of hours, we were given a sealed envelope of documents which we were to present at the American Embassy the next day. We were also required to present Luke in person at that appointment. At this point, with all the chaos in the city, there was no guarantee that the embassy would even be open the next day. It felt like Port-au-Prince was ready to implode at any moment. It felt like we were in a scene from one of those dystopian movies, where the main characters are running down the street just yards in front of the disaster overtaking the city behind them. If we didn't get Luke out of the city within the next few days, it was very likely we would be forced to leave him behind.

In faith that we would be able to present Luke at the American Embassy the next day, we picked him up from the orphanage the afternoon of the 17th. In my diary I wrote: "The nursery workers were both relieved and sad to see us come and hear that we were finally taking Luke with us. They all gathered around to say their goodbyes to Luke—he was obviously a favorite to them. Luke himself was, or seemed, almost happy to be leaving! He gave the nursery workers shy smiles when they kissed and patted him and did not seem alarmed or scared to be leaving. It was like he was thinking, 'FINALLY you guys are taking me! What took you so long!' One of the workers broke down and cried. That made me cry too. We asked for a bottle and formula to take with us. Luke also took the little stuffed bear that we had given him, and we took our family picture that we had taped to his crib. And then we walked out of the nursery for the last time."

I remember taking Luke to our borrowed jeep and buckling his little almost-2-year-old body in the backseat beside me (no car seats in this scenario). He did not cry or look back and just seemed resolute for whatever was to come. At the time, I was awed by his reaction and attributed his emotional state to a kind of personal ethereal inner strength or knowing that everything was going to be okay. Decades later, I wondered if instead this was a trauma response, a kind of shut-down, an emotionless protective mode. To this day, I'm not sure which it was.

February 18 — *from the Associated Press: "Haiti's Prime Minister warned Tuesday of an impending coup and appealed for international help to contend with a bloody uprising that has claimed 57 lives. But the United States and France expressed reluctance to send troops to put down the rebellion. Aid agencies called for urgent international action, warning Haiti is on 'the verge of a generalized civil war'. The UN refugee agency met with officials in Washington to discuss how to confront a feared exodus of Haitians. On Tuesday, airlines in Port-au-Prince canceled flights to the northern port of Cap-Haitien, Haiti's second-largest city, after witnesses in the barricaded city saw a boat approach and rumors swept the town that rebels were about to attack."*

Miraculously, the morning of February 18, we were at the American Embassy with Luke, documents in hand. As we were waiting for our appointment, an embassy employee came and sat with us in the waiting room and gave us a mini-lecture about how we should not be in Haiti in this dangerous time. She warned us that even the embassy people were getting ready to leave and we really should get out as soon as possible. We had already heard those things before, so we sort of nodded politely and determined to stay our course. The adoption process was almost complete, and we planned to be on a plane for home the next day.

Typically, the embassy would collect the visa paperwork during that morning appointment and ask the person to return in the afternoon to pick up the actual visa. However, with the chaos and instability in the city that day, there was no guarantee that the embassy would even be open that afternoon. So they expedited the process, and we received Luke's visa at 11:30am!

February 19 — We flew out of Haiti and back to Denver! Luke was a trooper on the plane. He slept a lot, and when he was awake, he loved to take the magazines out of the seatback pocket and rip the pages from top to bottom. We let him. We had a lot to discover about this little boy, who was a stranger to us and we to him. When we arrived in cold Denver and tried to put a coat on Luke, he cried and resisted so I carried him inside my coat as best I could. Of course his siblings and grandparents were thrilled to finally meet this little boy! But our joy was his overwhelm. We were all strangers to him, and this was a completely strange world he had been plunked into.

February 23 — Luke turns 2! Our family has a cake and presents and a party for him. He is not thrilled—again, our joy is his overwhelm. He does not want the cake and does not like the loud sounds of "Happy Birthday" sung and party horns tooted. One present in particular freaks him out—it's a toy car that can move and make sounds by itself. He is most happy playing with the little wooden cars made by Toys for God's Kids. We had brought probably 50 of them to Haiti for the kids in the orphanage and they had gone wild with them, sometimes doing the prescribed rolling across the floor, but more often loudly banging them on the floor! Luke was becoming an expert at rolling his. And we discovered he much preferred Maria cookies (a plain biscuit-like cookie) to the decadent birthday cake.

This same day, the rebels in Haiti successfully seized the northern city of Cap-Haitien and vowed to take Port-au-Prince.

February 29 — *from the Associated Press: " President Jean-Bertrand Aristide resigned and flew into exile Sunday, pressured by a bloody rebellion and the United States. Gunfire crackled as the capital [Port-au-Prince] fell into chaos, and the US Marines arrived in the country.*

The crisis has been brewing since Aristide's party swept flawed legislative elections in 2000, prompting international donors to freeze millions of dollars in aid. Opponents also accused Aristide of breaking promises to help the poor, allowing corruption and fueled by drug trafficking and masterminding attacks on opponents by armed gangs - charges the president denied. After word spread of Aristide's departure, angry Aristide supporters roamed the streets armed with old rifles, pistols, machetes and sticks. Some fired wildly into crowds on the Champs de Mars, the main square in front of the National Palace."

The Haitian Coup of 2004 is documented as possibly the most politically destabilizing event in that nation's history. Armed rebel gangs controlled the country until controversial foreign forces came in to attempt to restore order, or perhaps establish their own political control. In September of 2004, Haiti was hit by Tropical Storm Jeanne, causing flooding and the deaths of over 2000 people. Haiti continues to be a country buffeted by political and natural disasters: "mountains beyond mountains."

It is indeed a wonder that we were able to bring Luke out of Haiti during those days of the 2004 coup. Intellectually, we knew about the dangers surrounding us, but that knowledge didn't seem to affect the intention of our hearts. It was like we were living a separate reality, and the Universe was honoring our mission, in spite of the chaos all around.

Luke himself was a wonder...

I've always believed that Luke could've been anything he wanted to be. Anyone who knew him knew that Luke was exceptionally smart and able. In every way.

Academically, he was a math whiz. He loved languages. For the first two years of his life in Haiti he heard nothing but Creole. However, he picked up English within months. In first grade Luke asked me to make Spanish flashcards for him, and we bought a Spanish kids' Bible so he could learn Spanish. In high school he excelled in French. He was a great writer, even though he thought he wasn't. He loved to read. He could explain things methodically and clearly. I always thought he'd make a great teacher (in fact, he did tutor his classmates in math).

Socially, Luke knew how to make friends and influence people and maneuver socially. He was always very busy with all the relationships in his life. We always said he could be the president of Haiti one day.

Physically, Luke had energy up to wazoo. He seemed to excel in every sport he played, and he played a lot: T-ball, soccer, karate, basketball, cross-country running, hiking, climbing and parkour. There was a time when I thought he might play for the NBA—he was so smooth and natural on the court.

Artistically, Luke played the piano and trumpet. It seemed like no big deal for him to pick up a new instrument. He could draw and sketch.

And then there was general savvy-ness. I don't know quite how to describe this, but Luke had an uncanny ability to be very aware of all things at all times. It might be called a survival skill, a trauma response he learned as a young child. It made him an excellent employee in a fast-food setting. At 14 he was working at Chick-fil-A. At 16 he transitioned to Starbucks. We always thought he could easily have owned and managed his own franchise.

As far as capabilities go, I would describe Luke as a 2.0 version of a human being. Remarkable, considering his impoverished beginnings and severe malnourishment as an infant. It seemed like surviving all he did had made his brain and body extra strong and capable.

Signs

A strange thing happens when a person experiences deep grief. As my therapist, R, explained, it's like you're plunked into an alternate reality. "Normal" life is like a side-show; you're not invested in it anymore. It's happening around you, but it seems almost dream-like.

Maybe it's a kind of trauma response, this shutting off of day-to-day reality, this detachment. However, a wonderful side-effect of shutting down to the "normal" is that you become open to and aware of the "beyond normal", or what some may call the paranormal.

Balloon in the Bedroom

Turns out that many of us in our Coping After Suicide moms' group had paranormal experiences with our children after they passed. After having been together for some weeks in the group, as we grew more comfortable with and trusting of each other, those experiences began to be shared. I remember one mother describing how, not long after her son passed, she held a baby shower for her son's cousin. He was close with this cousin and surely would have been at the shower had he still been in physical form. After the party they cleaned up but left the helium balloons in the living room. The next morning, to this mom's surprise, one of the helium balloons was in her bedroom! It baffled her how the balloon had made its way from the living room, down the hallway, up the stairs, through the door and into her room. To her, it was a sign from her son that he was indeed a part of the celebration, even from the other side.

Baby Messenger

Another mom, T, shared that shortly after her son, Chance, died she was invited to speak, using his story, at a suicide prevention event that a friend of hers was hosting in another city. She went and was eager to participate but had some apprehension about whether her son would approve of her doing so. Was he okay with her sharing his story, and so soon? T spoke at the event and on the flight home happened to sit beside a young mother and her infant son. T was struck by how much the baby looked like her son when he was a baby with his blonde curly hair and even a dimple in the same left cheek. She and the young mom had a pleasant conversation and T helped with the baby here and there, holding him while the mom used the restroom, etc. When T asked the baby's name, she was shocked to hear it was Chance, the name of her son! T shared that then she knew this was her son making his presence known from the other side. For her, it was a sign that her son approved of her making this trip and sharing his story. Her angst was relieved and her heart comforted.

Finding the Christmas Angel

Especially in the first years after Luke died, I received several signs from him. Luke died in September. That Christmas I still felt like I was living in an alternate reality. I did manage to put up some Christmas decorations for the sake of my family. When he was younger, Luke was eager to help decorate the trees (we had more than one), especially our real tree with ornaments from all the places we'd been to around the world. I was particularly fond of the Philippine angel tree topper, made from abaca fiber, that we bought while living in Tacloban in 1994. It gave me joy to see it perched at the apex of the tree in all its creative simplicity—it was one of a kind. That Christmas others had bought and decorated the tree, and the angel was not on top. I went hunting for it and couldn't find it anywhere. It was missing, just like Luke, and its absence was adding to my despair. Christmas morning was warm and snow-free and I was the first one up, so I decided to walk the dogs. As I passed through the dining room, there on the floor was the Philippine angel. I was so thankful! Seems silly, but that little angel filled me with the comfort and joy of the season. I felt it was a Christmas gift from Luke to me.

Falling Pictures

I've been told that our loved ones who have passed are eager to give us signs, and that they often do so by manipulating light or small objects with their continuing energy. Like the balloon that appeared in the mom's bedroom. As a fourth-grader Luke had created what I like to think of as a mosaic kind of chicken, with various kinds of paper and patterns worked into it. I've always been tickled by that chicken. Going through his things after he passed, I had rediscovered his chicken art and sticky-tacked it to the outside of one of our dining room cupboard doors. Some weeks later, our family was sitting around the dining room table reminiscing/processing about Luke. As we were talking about him, the chicken art became unstuck and floated to the floor beside us. My husband D reacted with, "Okay, Luke, we know you're here!" That was the undeniable feeling in the room.

Around that same time I was cleaning the kitchen floor, near the stairwell going upstairs. I had baby photos of our four children sticky-tacked to the sloped ceiling above the steps, so I could see them as I came down from our upstairs bedroom every morning. On this particular afternoon, as I was cleaning the floor, I was thinking about Luke quite intensely. Right then his baby photo came unstuck, floated down and landed face up in front of me. What are the chances that out of the four baby photos Luke's was the photo that would become unstuck at that particular moment and land face up right in front of me? To me, it felt like a message from Luke: "Mom, I'm still right here."

Signs in the Sky

On September 17, 2022, the one-year anniversary of the day Luke transitioned, I took our dogs for a walk in the late afternoon in the park by our home. As we made our way down the straight-away cement path I looked up and there in the sky ahead of us was a single cloud with a fragment of a full-spectrum rainbow jutting out of it. All around, as far as I could see, the sky was blue and clear, no rain in sight. Within a few minutes the rainbow faded. It seemed perfectly timed and positioned for me to see. Seeing it filled me with a sense of peace and hope and comfort.

The next day I again walked the dogs, this time at night and in the opposite direction. It was a beautiful, fall, star-studded night. I looked up and happened to see a shooting star unlike any I had seen before. It left a long, distinct trail of dashed light behind it. I felt privileged to witness it. It felt like a gift, like I had been lucky to see it. It felt like another gift from Luke. (In the months and years that followed, the idea of stars and light would become increasingly significant in their association with Luke. More on that later in the book...)

Cell Phone Signs

Our family shares a cell phone plan, and in January of 2023 it was time to upgrade our phones. The now five of us coordinated our schedules (not an easy proposition at that time) and met at the Verizon store one weekday afternoon. As we were all sitting at the counter going through the tedious process of contracting our new phones, a young man came up beside us. The store clerk asked his name, and he replied, "Luke." The clerk couldn't seem to find him in the system and repeated his name, "Luke," three or four times for clarification. Finally, the young man said, "You might not find me with that name." So why did he let the store clerk flounder with what seemed to be the wrong name for a prolonged period of time? To me, this was another sign from Luke, fitting of his mischievous nature, reminding us that he was still around. Also, Luke's cell phone had been his most prized possession in this life, so it was very appropriate that he'd choose a cell-phone store where we were all gathered to make his presence known!

Speaking of cell phones, I've learned that our loved ones on the other side will often use technology to speak to us. The sensitivity of technology makes it relatively easy for spirit to manipulate. I remember one day in the first months after Luke's passing, my phone randomly created a Facebook memory slide show exclusively of him. Luke was born on February 23. A couple of days before his birthday on 2/23/2023, I went to set the alarm on my cell phone and found it set for a strange 23 minutes. The morning of his birthday that year, I opened my phone and it was saying "hi" in multiple languages, over and over again. Turns out my phone had updated itself during the night. I didn't remember giving my permission for the update and it seemed uncanny (and like

Luke) that I'd receive those "hello" messages that particular morning. Maybe Luke orchestrated the update for that particular night?

A couple of days later I was reading Hollister Rand's book *I'm Not Dead, I'm Different* and happened to be on the chapter "Bringing Heaven Home: How Kids Say Hi." I read that kids in spirit "use technology to say hi" (p.233)! How much more literal could the message be, as my phone had literally said "hi" the morning of Luke's birthday? As I kept reading, and asking Luke, "Was that really you?" I happened upon the following sentence: "One mother has no doubt that her son, Luke, is saying 'hello'" (p.234). What are the chances?! I got goosebumps and finally let the idea that my Luke was saying "hi" settle on my soul.

Dad Signs

Exactly a year and a half after Luke passed, my dad passed. My dad had been suffering, unknowingly, with pancreatic cancer probably up to a year before he passed. Finally, when he was unable to bear the pain in his belly any longer, he acquiesced to being admitted to the hospital. He would never return home. My dad's last days in the hospital were filled with stress and uncertainty as the doctors ordered various tests to diagnose his illness. He ended up dying in the hospital while waiting for a bed to open in hospice care. I'm explaining all of this to highlight that the timing of my dad's death was unexpected and unpredictable. However, the night of the day of his passing I was lying in bed and realized that it was Friday, the 17th of the month, and dad had passed at 7:35am. Luke had also passed on a Friday, the 17th of the month, at 7:35am. The similarities seemed uncanny. And somehow comforting. Like what seemed random wasn't actually so random.

Like there was a larger plan and pattern. More particularly, it felt like a sign to me that my dad and Luke were together, syncing up to point us to a larger reality. The synchronized timing also made me wonder if Luke was helping to welcome my dad to his home on the other side, as dad had helped to welcome Luke into our earthly home.

A few months later, my step-mom told me an amazing story about her hearing aid. She only has one since her other ear is too deaf to be helped by a hearing aid. My dad cared a LOT about that hearing aid. Probably, one, because it cost $2000 and my step-mom was often losing or misplacing it. And probably, two, because it was frustrating to try to communicate with her with two nearly-deaf ears. He was constantly asking my step-mom if she had her hearing aid in, even as he lay dying in his hospital bed! In the weeks after dad died, my step-mom again lost her hearing aid. She looked all over for it, retracing her steps around the retirement village where she lives, asking friends, etc. No luck. Then, a few days later, in the rain, as she was walking back to her condo from an event in another building she happened to look down at the sidewalk, and there was her hearing aid! She took it home, wiped it off, put it in her ear, and it worked! What are the chances that her hearing aid would have survived completely intact on the sidewalk in the rain for three days, that she would happen to see it, and on top of that, that it would still work! To me, that was a sign from dad, that he is still with my step-mom, helping her. I can just imagine him saying, "Okay, hon," (short for "honey", which he always called her) "here it is. Now put it in!" My step-mom recently told me that she has now lost her hearing aid *four* times and found it again every time!

Signs Revisited

In early February 2025, a few days before my birthday, I was writing the section "Experiencing Luke's Death" in this book. Malte Marten's handpan music on YouTube has been my constant listening companion while writing this entire book. My habit is to find one of his videos and let YouTube's random selection take it from there. It's all Malte Marten (usually) but in no particular order and I have no idea what's coming next.

After writing that particular section I decided to take a lunch break and clicked on the YouTube tab to pause the music video. To my surprise, the title of the current randomly-selected video I had been inadvertently listening to was "For My Parents." It had been released last year on February 23, the date of Luke's birthday. Malte noted it was fitting to release this video in February because both of his parents' birthdays are in February. As I mentioned, my birthday is also in February.

To me, having that particular video appear at that particular time felt like a gift and sign from Luke. I believe he was witnessing me writing about that hard time, recalling those hard memories, and wanted to show his support. What are the chances that that particular video, with all those specific connections, would appear at that moment?

Much like Malte Marten's handpan music, I feel like Luke is always in the background, inspiring and encouraging me as I write. "For My Parents." A birthday gift from Luke to me.

Signs or Coincidences?

It's a fair question, and probably one that many of you may be asking. I suppose it depends on your perspective. What appears to be a sign to one may appear to be a mere coincidence to another.

For me, I can agree that often a sign *is* a coincidence. It's a coincidence that occurs at a perfect moment and becomes a message. A sign doesn't even have to be a coincidence. The sun coming up every day is a sign that life on earth is still worth it. The fact that we can take a breath is a sign that we still have life to live. A passerby sharing a smile is a sign that there is still love and goodwill in the world.

We are surrounded by signs and wonders every day, both common and uncommon. Whether we pause long enough to appreciate the messages is up to us.

LESSON THREE

Love Matters Most

I wish I was better at love. There are some people that just exude it. I believe we all have love inside but some of us have a harder time uncovering it and letting it out.

Love Lessons with Celebrate Recovery

In 2011, ten years before Luke passed, I joined Celebrate Recovery (CR), the Christian version of the 12 Steps.

I was not an alcoholic. I was a good Christian mother of four, a former missionary, volunteer extraordinaire both in the church and in my children's schools. In retrospect, maybe I was a "good-aholic." Or maybe a "serve-aholic."

All I knew, back in 2011, was that I was depressed. Most days I felt like a hamster in a wheel, racing to keep everything together but not really going anywhere. I was exhausted, feeling trapped and even victimized in my role as a wife and mother. I felt like a failure, like I had made bad life-decisions and had missed God's calling on my life. Somehow, I needed to start over. I started praying that God would show me the truth about my life, and that if something needed to be changed in me, would He please change it.

Several years before I joined CR, I experienced another vivid dream of the same quality and "realness" (and as comforting) as the bird dream with Luke. In this dream, I was sitting in a circle of women with an African American woman leading. We were all sharing our stories. Even though at that time I had no personal experience with the 12 Steps, I knew it was that kind of group. It was a nice dream but that was all. I didn't struggle with drugs or alcohol, so what could a group like that have to do with me?

When I was actually confronted, in 2011, with the real possibility of joining CR, I was scared. Scared to face my own crap, probably. I had to write down, with pen and paper, all the reasons I was going to do this (an inner push/conviction, a possible way out of my depression, I wanted to be a better, healed mom and person) so I wouldn't back out. Then, one day, in the middle of the afternoon, as I bent over to pick something off the kitchen floor, that recurring dream about the AA meeting came back to me in all its vividness. I was convicted and brought to tears. This was the final confirmation/push I needed. I was sure this CR women's group opportunity was for me.

Turns out my CR group, as in my dream, was led by an African American woman. And all five of us participants in the group were adoptive mothers.

I've often thought back to the advice one of those mothers gave me, as I was tearfully expressing my frustrations with parenting Luke. He was our youngest child and the most challenging. She said, "Next time you have a conflict with Luke, just grab him and hug him!" I could never gather within myself whatever it took to do that. I was so angry in those moments that the last thing I felt like doing, or even *thought* of doing, was grabbing my son and hugging him! Looking back, I wonder what a difference that might have made if I had been able to give those hugs. If the most fundamental message Luke had received, no matter what conflict we were having, was "I love you," physically communicated so he could feel it in his body, viscerally. And I wonder what a difference it would have made for me, to physically move my body beyond my anger, beyond the constriction and tightness of self-protection, to open arms embracing the pain of my son. How would that have shifted my heart and mind to a new perspective in those volatile moments?

Self-Love

On one level, it was the challenge of parenting Luke that drove me to a point of desperation and the 12 Steps. However, on a deeper level, I think my own lack of self-love brought me there.

As a devoted Christian, Matthew 22:37 served as a kind of true north for me throughout my life: "Love the Lord your God with all your heart, soul and mind, and love your neighbor as yourself." Jesus said that sentence summed up all the law and the prophets, and I like boiling things down to simple truths that I can remember and follow. However, I'm not sure that I ever fully understood the message of that verse. I think the syntax threw me off. "As yourself" is added at the end, almost like an after-thought. It doesn't appear central to the formula.

For years I was running on empty, dutifully serving God and others, as I was taught and conditioned to do, with no real regard or awareness of myself. I thought that was an honorable way to live the Christian life: denying the self and putting others' needs before my own. In those days I couldn't have told you what I wanted or what gave me joy or what my dreams were. I had lost myself. I was running around putting oxygen masks on everyone else (even on God, I think) without realizing I didn't have a mask on myself. I was feeling more and more depleted, which led me to resent the people I was serving (mostly my family). That resentment made me feel trapped in my role as a wife and mother; it made me feel like a victim of my circumstances. And yet I was the one who had chosen this life for myself, so there was no one to blame but me. I was caught in a vicious cycle of unhappiness and self-blame.

In addition, I didn't like what I saw in myself as I parented Luke. I had never known myself to be such an angry person. I felt like the Incredible Hulk, the guy in the 1977 Sci-fi TV series, who was mild-mannered in daily life but would turn into a raging green monster when triggered. Luke was my trigger-master—it was like he instinctively knew how to push my buttons. I've heard it said that the people who trigger us the most are our greatest teachers—they are like mirrors revealing our shadow-side, forcing us to deal with the stuff we'd rather keep hidden. Luke certainly did that for me. I didn't like the angry, reactive parent I had become.

Reflecting back, I think CR did at least two big things for me. One, it helped me drop the facade of "being good." I learned that it's okay to be kind of a screw-up. Being a part of a supportive community filled with struggling people like me, where we could just be honest about our sh**, accept it, and come to terms with it, felt like a breath of fresh air. I felt like, "Ahhhh, these are my people!" Our struggles may have been different, but we were not denying them any longer, and there was a cumulative sense of relief in our mutual release.

Two, CR helped restore my sense of self. Upon my completion of the 12 Steps I was honored with the opportunity to lead a version of the 12 Steps for teens. Others seeing the leadership potential in me and entrusting me with this new program for teens awakened my own spirit. I was filled with an inexplicable energy for the work. Showing up every single Friday night for a year never felt like a burden. Even on nights when attendance was low, I did not feel disheartened. Whatever came, came—I was just happy to be part of it all. This ministry filled my tank like nothing had for a long time. I felt like I was coming back to myself. I was in the flow and following my joy. I will forever be grateful for that experience. (The teen program also gave me a precious new friendship with K, my co-leader. It meant so much to me, a decade later, when K read the Serenity Prayer at Luke's memorial.)

I was 44 when I joined CR. Luke was 9 at the time. Even though we were at very different life stages I think we were both suffering from the same ailment: a lack of self-love. Luke went beyond a lack of love to actual disdain for himself. I remember once our whole family of six met with Luke's therapist for a session. At one point, sort of impromptu, we went around and said what we appreciated about Luke: his sense of smarts, his energy, his athletic ability, his creative/artistic ability, the way he could charm and influence people, etc. It seemed the more we shared positive characteristics, the angrier Luke got. He just could not receive those things, maybe especially not from the people closest to him.

Luke was also a master of self-sabotage. He would want to do something, work hard at it and be good at it, but when it came time to put his skills to the test, he would flake out or quit in the face of competition. For example, he liked karate and excelled at it in the gym but in competitions he was never able to show what he could do. In school, he was very smart academically but would do poorly on tests or refuse to turn in assignments. He was a star on his YMCA basketball team but would turn sullen and angry if his team lost, thinking everyone was blaming him for the loss. It felt to me like he was never able to fully step into and enjoy the multitude of gifts and abilities he was blessed with. He was always haunted by feelings of unworthiness, of not being enough. Any kind of failure only exacerbated those feelings; consequently, if there was a chance of failure, he would usually reject the opportunity.

If Luke had loved himself, I believe he would still be on this earth today. I'm not saying that's the case for everyone who passes by suicide, but for Luke, I think his main challenge in this life was to learn how to accept and appreciate himself. And I wish I could've role-modeled that better for him.

What is self-love? It's fully accepting myself, in this moment, with all my faults and failures, just as I am right now. Not withholding my love until I lose 20 pounds, or until I achieve that promotion at work, or until I prove myself or change myself in some way. Not withholding my love because I've done something I can't forgive myself for. It's being able to look in the mirror and say, "I love you." Self-love is gratitude for my amazing self! Gratitude that I was given the opportunity to be in this particular body, at this particular time, experiencing my unique life on earth, whatever that may be. Self-love is grounded in reality: I acknowledge that I'm a work in progress and so I embrace opportunities for growth and expansion. I'm not threatened by my shadow side, and I don't need to deny or cover up anything because I love all parts of myself, trusting that life is making me better, like time improves a fine wine or cheese.

Recently I walked the Camino, a 155-mile pilgrimage in Europe.

Our guide (shout out to Laura Harris and Pilgrim Paths) was full of stories about how various Caminos that she had walked (there are many in Europe and around the world) had influenced her life. Recounting her first solo Camino, she told us how she had called her husband and said, "I'm walking with this wonderful person who likes everything I like, wants to go to the same places I want to go, and has deep conversations with me—I'm having such a great time with her!" That's self-love. Not arrogance, but an authentic appreciation of myself. Like I'm my best friend.

I've come to learn that I can't authentically love others, God included, if I don't authentically love myself. I can't give what I don't have. Learning to accept and forgive my own faults allows me to accept and forgive the faults of others. When I can appreciate myself as I am right now, I can learn to appreciate others as they are right now. I can love God and others out of my own abundance rather than out of some unconscious (or conscious) need for self-fulfillment.

For most of us, this is a life-long struggle, to learn how to authentically appreciate and accept ourselves. Most of us never quite get there. But Luke has taught me that self-love is essential to life itself.

Cauldron of Self-Love

I was exposed to and learned so much while working with sex-trafficked adolescent girls at Resilience Rising. I will always be grateful for that experience. I was privileged to attend various excellent trauma trainings during that time. One presenter likened treating trauma to making a salad. There is trauma in the bowl but by adding more and different ingredients, the effect of the trauma can be diminished. As you make the salad bigger, the effect of the trauma decreases. Likewise, as we add different positive experiences into our lives, like pursuing hobbies, developing skills, serving others, etc., our trauma can be neutralized.

I'd like to change the analogy from salad to a big pot (or cauldron) of chili. Trauma is the spice. If there's too much spice, the chili becomes unpalatable. No need to throw out the chili, just add more ingredients until that perfect blend is achieved.

Essential to this process is having a big enough pot to contain all the added ingredients. Self-love is that container for us. It's what holds all our stuff, the spice and the beans, the "bad" and the "good." The more love we have for ourselves, the more we can contain *all* of what life gifts us.

Puppy Love

Soon after Luke died, we made what some call a "grief purchase": buying something way out of the normal budget to help fill the hole or lessen the sorrow after a loved one passes. Our particular grief purchase was a $2000 mini Goldendoodle from a reputable breeder in Pennsylvania (shout-out to Crockett Doodles). We named her Canella, mimicking the Spanish word for cinnamon, in acknowledgement of her beautiful rusty-brown color. In true puppy fashion, Canella did indeed bring us comfort and joy in our early months of grieving. On a deeper level, I think caring for all her puppy needs somehow helped my subconscious compensate for not being able to take care of Luke the way I would have wanted to: in his final days, at the point of his death, and really throughout his life with us. I wasn't there like I wanted to be for Luke, but I could be there for Canella. For weeks I slept beside her crate on a foamie on the floor in our family room while she was being potty-trained. I bought a front-pack carrier for her so I could take her with me wherever I went. I kind of devoted my life to her for a time—seems a bit crazy now, but it was what I needed then, and I was and continue to be grateful for Canella's presence in our lives.

Turns out Canella is the embodiment of unconditional love. Nothing gives her more joy than loving on people. It doesn't matter the size, color, gender, or emotional state of the person in her path—she runs up to everyone with joyful abandon, greeting every person like her long-lost friend. It's interesting to watch people's reactions, from "Oh yes, I have a way with dogs, they like me" to "Why am I so special?" to no words but just a smile on a weary face. Canella lights people up. It's hard to resist her friendliness. She just naturally spreads joy.

It's hard for most of us humans to love like that. Canella's a constant role-model.

LESSON FOUR

What We Do Is Not Who We Are

This is a hard one. In western capitalistic society so much of our identity is wrapped up in what we do and the roles we play. And our value is measured by how much we produce or contribute.

Luke's life and death has continually challenged me to let go of the roles I identify with and to value myself beyond what I do.

Letting Go of My "Mom" Identity

For most of my life, if someone were to ask me who I was or what I did, I would say I was a mom, and eventually a mom of four. I loved (and love) my children and dedicated all my time and energy for many years to raising them. I thought I was a pretty good mom and enjoyed seeing my kids grow and develop. At the same time, I often felt bad and "less than" because I wasn't earning money for the family (even though my husband was bringing in a good wage), and because I was "just a mom" with no real professional identity or aspirations.

My feelings of inadequacy in limiting my role to motherhood became intensified as Luke grew up. As I said, I thought I was a pretty good mom, until we were blindsided with behaviors from Luke that we had no idea how to deal with. The limits we set with our other children did not work for him. We were dumbfounded as to how to parent a child who defied the rules and raged when we tried to enforce them, who blatantly lied to our faces, who refused to join in family activities, who would run away from home. Many times, I did not know how to be a mother to Luke. I felt useless in that role. And I was not proud of my angry and frustrated reactions to him.

On top of that, I felt rejected by Luke. No matter how hard I tried to make him happy, by enrolling him in a multitude of activities, finding him good schools, connecting him with relatable therapists, etc., nothing seemed to reach him. At some point I decided to stop trying so hard. When Luke was in high school we decided, for our own sanity, to basically let him do what he wanted and to stop keeping tabs on him. I felt like I had basically abdicated my role as his mother. He was our youngest and the only one living at home at that time, so I shed that day-to-day mothering role. It didn't feel good, but it felt like survival.

Before I completely dissolved into a pile of uselessness, I decided to turn my focus outward and continue on a path I had been on decades ago, before marriage and children, the path of professional social work. At age 48 I was delighted to be accepted into a Master of Social Work program. Four years later I graduated with my Master of Social Work degree.

Letting Go of Titles

After graduating with my Master of Social Work in 2019 and becoming a Licensed Social Worker (LSW) with the state in 2020, my next professional goal was to become a Licensed Clinical Social Worker (LCSW). In 2021, when Luke passed, I was well on my way to gaining the clinical hours I needed through my job as a trauma-informed caregiving trainer for adoptive and foster families.

However, when Luke died, I also lost my job. Basically, my program director decided that after experiencing the trauma of my own adopted son passing by suicide, I was no longer able to do my job. I remember her saying to me, in the where-do-we-go-from-here conversation we had just a week or so after Luke passed: "In your gut, you know what you need to do." She repeated it at least three times in the course of our rather brief conversation. I got the message: "Please step down." I was also told, "We can give you three months leave with pay." Perhaps an additional concern was that my less-than-optimal experience with my adopted son would tarnish the reputation of the organization. Later I learned the grant funding for my position had also been lost right around that time. Regardless of all the rationales, getting that message felt like a gut punch. The loss of my job, in addition to the loss of my son, felt surreal. Was this really happening? It felt like everything was tumbling down around me.

Earlier I mentioned my therapist—remember the woman, R, I had sought out for career counseling (before Luke passed) who also happened to specialize in grief counseling? During one of our sessions several months after Luke's passing, R told me that the career path I was on had "blown up." Blown up?! I remember being somewhat shocked that she declared that so directly and emphatically. Usually, R was all about gently guiding me to come to my own conclusions. Blown up?! How could that be, after I had invested so much time, money and energy into getting my MSW, my LSW and now hopefully my LCSW? I was working as hard as I could, pursuing a career that I felt was in line with my gifts and skills, with a passion to serve others. It made no sense for that to blow up. It couldn't blow up. I was too invested. And I felt like I was finally doing something that I was made for, something larger than my role as a wife, mother, volunteer, and special education paraprofessional (all vital roles, but these were my feelings at the time). It felt cruel for the Universe to take this away from me too, even while I was grieving the loss of my son!

So, I rejected that scenario. About a year and a half after Luke passed, I decided to gather up whatever scattered pieces were left of my professional path and try my hardest to put it back together. I was offered two internships that would credit me clinical hours in exchange for working voluntarily. Wonderful! I chose to work as a social-emotional teacher at a bilingual elementary school. It was a good decision. I felt supported and challenged and like I was building on the skills I had. I was even given the opportunity to lead a grief group for children—something I felt very comfortable with since I was now very familiar with grief. However, about four months into the internship it became clear that the organization I was volunteering for (not the school itself) was not able to offer me the clinical hours or supervision they had promised me. This was a new program and those in charge had not fully understood the requirements of my LCSW hours. Wow, another unforeseen setback. What was going on?! However, I was thankful for the experience and the wonderful children and team I had learned from and with. I ended my term of volunteer service there early, in search of another position that would give me those clinical hours.

Thankfully, the internship I had turned down the first time was willing to re-interview me and hired me! I would be working on a farm that used therapy animals to work with children. This felt like a dream fulfilled! At this point, the window of time I had to complete my clinical hours was shrinking rapidly. However, I did the calculations and, with the hours I had accumulated in my previous job, it was possible for me to collect all that I needed in this internship. I contacted my clinical supervisor from the previous job to get his official approval for the hours we had agreed on. I was a little taken aback when he asked for proof of those hours. But I had kept records, so I sent those to him. Then came another curve ball. He informed me that he needed to renege on about half of the hours we had agreed on, since, in retrospect, those didn't qualify as "clinical." He reminded me that I had been the first LSW he had supervised, and he was learning too. You've got to be kidding me. My calculations were nullified—I would not be able to complete my clinical hours in the time frame allowed. So, I turned down the farm internship for a second time.

It felt like my LCSW dreams were slowly slipping through my clenched fingers. Maybe my therapist was right and that path had indeed blown up. It appears I had to experience that reality for myself, rather than simply hearing it from my therapist. If I'm honest, all along I had had my own misgivings about being a "professional social worker." I guess my therapist had picked up on those. In fact, the reason I started seeing her, before Luke died, was because of my angst over those misgivings. However, after Luke died, I was looking for things to hold on to. I had lost my son. I had lost my job. The LCSW path was still a possibility. Maybe it could help me find my footing once again. Now it seemed I was losing that too.

Canella Teaching Me That It's Okay to Let Go

At the time of this writing, Canella is three years old. She was indeed a grief purchase, but I also had a long-time dream of having a therapy dog that I could use with kids, and a mini Goldendoodle seemed like the perfect breed. About a year ago Canella and I made a go at volunteering as a therapy team with Pet Partners. Unfortunately, Canella's "vocalizing" and over-enthusiasm during the first three minutes of the very formal testing disqualified us for service. I have to admit I was very disappointed—you might say pissed—at our immediate disqualification after all the time and money I had invested in the process. On a deeper level, I felt it was another blow to my professional career, another blocking of my desire to serve traumatized kids as an LCSW.

I was clearly upset that we failed the therapy dog test, but Canella was not at all (of course she wasn't—she's a dog and has simple needs: love and treats). After failing the test, I needed to walk off some steam so I took Canella to a nearby park. A young woman walked toward us on the path, and, in her usual fashion, Canella wriggled and lunged up towards her on the leash, like this woman was her long-lost best friend. Turns out this woman felt like Canella was indeed her long-lost friend! While enjoying all the love between them, the woman told me that her own dog had recently died and he was a Golden too, and she felt so comforted by Canella's affection. I had been feeling heart-broken and actually pissed off that Canella couldn't be a therapy dog and help all the sad people out there. But here she was doing just that, without the title. She was just herself, out in the world, bringing joy. No title necessary.

I think I've been hung up on titles. Somehow, to be able to say, "I'm a social worker, I'm an LSW, I'm an LCSW" gives me credibility, with the world and with myself. It sends the message that I've done something with my life, something that's recognized as valuable in society. So then maybe I can start to see the value in myself. *That's* what's hard to let go of. That self-imposed stamp of external approval.

Canella doesn't seem to need that. She just lets her light shine, no matter the circumstance, no worry about anyone's approval or disapproval (and there *are* a few who do not appreciate her hyper-love). She doesn't need to pass a test to be a therapy dog—she simply *is* one.

Margaret

When I was in middle school my friend C and I would sometimes visit a young lady named Margaret. Margaret went to our church, faithfully, every Sunday. That in itself was quite remarkable since Margaret's father, himself in his 60s, would have to carry her 30-something-year-old body up the outside flight of some 30 concrete steps to enter the church. Margaret lived at home and received around-the-clock care from her parents. Her body was permanently contorted in such a way that she was not able to sit up, much less feed, bathe, or toilet herself. She communicated with grunts and half-yells AND with her infectious, wide, beautiful smile.

I know Margaret had her moments. She would get upset and let people know it. But most often, at least how I remember it, Margaret was smiling. She would be thrilled when my friend and I came to visit her, her whole body shaking with excitement and her throat uttering guttural sounds of joy. She had a ready sense of humor and what I most remember from those visits was laughing together at something funny C or I would say, or laughing with Margaret when she would accidentally spill her food or knock something over (which happened frequently since parts of her body would uncontrollably and unpredictably spasm).

When I think back to Margaret and her parents, I'm amazed. The dedication, perseverance, and grace required to bear with all the challenges they faced together was, and is, inspiring. More than that, there was no question that Margaret's was a life worth living. She could do little else but lie in bed, smile and convey a few basic emotions. She was completely dependent on her parents to keep her alive day to day. Margaret couldn't "do" anything, couldn't produce anything, couldn't "prove" her value in this world. And yet there she was, smiling and laughing and receiving the love and devotion of her parents. Just by laying there and being Margaret.

You've probably heard it said that we are human *beings*, not human *doings*. How often do I/we allow ourselves to rest in our "being"-ness, trusting that our mere existence is proof that we can and should be here on planet earth? We don't have to prove ourselves worthy by getting that promotion, or landing that job, or buying that expensive _____, or having perfect grades, hair, bodies, partners, or kids. The truth is we are loved just as we are. It's a hard concept to grasp. It is for me; it was for Luke. Maybe thinking of Margaret can help us.

Ferdinand the Bull

When my oldest daughter was in first grade and we were living overseas, I decided to venture into home-schooling. For me, it was fun. For my daughter, not so much.

During that year we became acquainted with Ferdinand the Bull and his story of being recruited for the bullfights in Madrid, Spain. Normally Ferdinand was a very easy-going, simple-minded kind of bull, content to sit under the cork tree smelling the flowers. One day, when he went to sit in his favorite spot under the tree, he inadvertently sat right on a bee who stung him hard in self-defense. Understandably, Ferdinand shot up and started stomping and screaming and flaring his nostrils—carrying on like a madman (or madbull, in this case). This of course was completely out of character for this normally mild-mannered, happy bull. Unfortunately, right as Ferdinand was in the middle of his bee-sting tirade, the bull-fight recruiters happened to come by. The behavior Ferdinand was displaying was perfect for a bull fight! So, they excitedly hauled him off to Madrid to compete. However, once in the bull ring, Ferdinand saw and smelled all the lovely flowers in the fancy hats of the spectating ladies, reverted back to his true self, and sat placidly in the middle of the ring, content to enjoy all the wafting floral scents surrounding him. Embarrassed and angry, the bull fight recruiters sent Ferdinand packing back to his home and his cork tree.

Anyone who knew Ferdinand could've advised the recruiters that Ferdinand was not the fighting bull they were looking for. But because they happened to see Ferdinand at the particular moment of the bee sting fiasco, and the type of *behavior* he was displaying was what they were focused on and wanted, they assumed *he* was the bull they wanted. However, Ferdinand's behavior at that moment was not a reflection of his character. What he did, how he behaved, was not who he was.

This is a hard concept for most of us to wrap our minds around. Generally, we are quick to judge "bad" behavior as indicative of bad character. What if, instead, bad behavior is indicative of the pain we're in? Bruce Perry wrote a book entitled *What Happened to You?* In it, he encourages his readers, when faced with the challenging behavior of others, to replace the question, "Why did you do that?!" with "What happened to you?" As in the case of Ferdinand, the "bad" things we do are an expression of the pain we're in, the trauma we've experienced, the suffering we hold on to. As they say, "Hurt people hurt people."

It makes sense that we would have the behavioral challenges we did with Luke, considering what he had come through and was carrying with him. As an infant he almost died of malnutrition, stayed in a hospital for months for recovery, lived in an orphanage for a year, then was removed from Haiti and brought to a stranger's house in a foreign country, and then was raised as a black male in a mostly white family and a largely hostile culture. Makes sense that all of that would come out in some behaviors.

I wish I could say that I carried this understanding into all my interactions with Luke and always approached him in a trauma-informed way. I did not. However, I did know, deep within me, that the behaviors we were dealing with were not who Luke was at his core. At his core, Luke was a bright, smart, hard-working, sincere, helpful, compassionate, sensitive, and generous person. It both broke my heart and infuriated me that we couldn't seem to get to that Luke for what felt like such a long time.

More Than What We Do

Beyond our roles, beyond our titles, beyond our "bad" behavior, we just are. It's a challenge to simply be. To accept that just being is okay. Even if we do nothing, our existence on this planet is justified. Even if we behave in ways we're not proud of, we belong here.

On every level, we are more than what we do. On every level, what we do does not have to define us.

LESSON FIVE

Our Triggers Can Heal Our Trauma

You may have heard it said that those who trigger us the most have the most to teach us. When we're bothered by another's behavior, it's likely that we are reacting to those same tendencies in ourselves, perhaps rejecting those behaviors or attitudes in ourselves. Or, another's behavior triggers some trauma wound from our past that we are not aware of or have not fully explored or integrated. It's like these bothersome people are holding a mirror in front of us, forcing us to face our own pain and faults. Their presence in our lives is actually a gift. But it sure doesn't feel that way. The process of self-discovery can be painful.

Fortunately, or unfortunately, these triggering, mirror-holding people are often those we share a roof with—our partners or family members. Luke was certainly that for me.

The Traumas We Shared

We walked through life looking like opposites: Luke black, me white.
We had unequal status: Luke the child, me the parent.
Some might say we were worlds apart: Luke Haitian, me Canadian/
American.

Under the geography, under the roles, under the skin, we had trauma in
common.

Luke's trauma was evident to some; mine was hidden.

Or maybe not ... my trauma, like Luke's, sometimes leaked out in wild behaviors and intense emotions that seemed to be outside of my control, making my reactions way out of sync with events.

Abandonment, the foundational trauma.

Luke had no choice but to carry abandonment around like a poster child, quite literally. His black face with our parental white ones broadcasted the story that his biological parents "gave him up." Never mind what a heart-wrenching decision that might have been. Never mind how inescapable the trap of poverty. Never mind the prose below the headline. "Gave Him Up" is all that outsiders had time to read. And it was the bold message that became imprinted on Luke's subconscious.

Someone would have to ask for my story to discover my trauma. My dad abandoned me when I was 7 years old. Not in his heart, not by his will, but by a decision of the courts. And then by the decision of my mom who married an abusive man and moved me and my sister hundreds of miles away from my dad, as far as the courts would allow. My relationship with my dad was reduced to handwritten letters (no internet at that time), phone calls, and holiday visits.

Trauma experts will admonish us not to compare traumas—mine worse than yours, or yours worse than mine. We each experience trauma uniquely, and we validate each experience, regardless of our tendency to judge degrees. That said, I want to acknowledge Luke's trauma as deeper than my own. The self he was born into was completely stripped away, his original identity all but erased. Luke never had the experience of looking into a relative's face and recognizing himself there: "Ah, that's where I got my smile!" He never saw himself mirrored, and consequently validated, by anyone familiar to him. On top of that, he was abruptly removed from his country, his language, his culture. At two years old he was completely unanchored, thrown into a completely unfamiliar world. He lost everything he had known, and in many ways lost the self he had just begun to form. His whole foundation abandoned him.

Wounds of mistrust. If our biological parent(s) could leave us, if our foundational relationships could crumble, both Luke and I learned on a subconscious level that no relationship is stable and trustworthy. How could he absolutely trust me? How could I absolutely trust him? The relationship was not guaranteed. We both had to see, every day, how things played out, and maybe build trust from there. Trust based on performance. That's a lot of pressure to put on a relationship. Because I can't trust, I need to protect myself, be the first to bail if I get any inkling that the other person might leave me. Or maybe hold on too tight, craving security and connection. Or vacillating between the two: "I love you/I hate you." Ambivalence. Like Luke participating in family activities but then making them miserable for everyone. Like me wanting to love Luke with all my heart one day and wanting to totally give up on him the next.

Wounds of a lost sense of self. My childhood was disrupted. Luke's was abducted. Both traumas had an impact on our developing selves. I would grow into self-deprecation. Luke would grow into self-loathing. Luke not appreciating and outright rejecting my efforts to support him would pour salt into the wound of me already not appreciating myself. Me confronting Luke about lying or not doing his best would pour salt into the wound of him already loathing himself. Normal behaviors of kids testing the

73

boundaries and parents correcting were not tolerated on either end. Normal felt painful and threatening.

Wounds of shame. The story of abandonment is not one to be proud of. Who stands up and says, "I am proud to have been abandoned by my parents?"

It feels shameful. Like a secret to be hidden. Like something bad, like maybe *I'm* bad.

Ashamed of our history, our roots, the brokenness that we came from.

We don't and can't measure up to those who came from wholeness.

Maybe some families can hide their brokenness—we cannot. It's in the court records and in the awkward explanations we are forced to give when people ask about our weird families.

We end up carrying shame around as a constant burden. Makes it hard to believe we really have something to offer in the world and in relationships. Makes it easy to take offense at any hint or comment that we might have something to improve on. Like how I feel defeated and angry when Luke runs to other "mamas," as if I'm not quite doing it for him. Like how Luke rages when I try to help him with his homework, as if he's stupid and not capable of doing it on his own.

These are the traumas Luke and I shared, at least the ones I'm able to acknowledge as I write this. I believe my healing will continue, and that Luke continues to help me from the other side. Not as a mirror like he once was, reflecting back to me what needed to be transformed, but as a mentor, gently guiding me into truth as I'm ready.

Cleansing the Mirror

I like the mirror analogy when it comes to thinking about healing. Cleansing our own mirrors/doing our own healing work enables us to be more objective in our interactions with others, more clear-headed and heart-centered. We become more able to respond instead of react, as they say.

Crystal Derksen, in her healing sessions with me, would systematically take me back to upsetting or traumatic situations and ask, "What is bothering you about this scenario?" Whatever I was bothered about was the clue to what still needed healing within me. Our triggers are like the "beep, beep!" of a metal detector, signaling that there's something below the surface, in our subconscious, that needs to be brought to the light and be healed.

It's important to keep our own mirrors clean so that they can offer accurate reflections to others. I read once that the goal of healing is to "perceive things as they are, not as I am." How often do we take offense at what someone says or does when no offense was intended? Or take a minor incident and blow it up into a major one? That happened a lot with Luke and I, to the extent that eventually interacting with each other felt like walking through a field of landmines, each of us just watching for the next explosion. I ask, "Did you do your homework?" Explosion from Luke. Luke asks, "Can you give me a ride?" Explosion from me. Seemingly innocuous questions. Out-of-proportion reactions. Obviously, there was a lot going on below the surface. Lots of resentment and anger and unresolved issues between us. There were many layers of dust and gunk clouding perceptions on both sides so that a simple question could no longer be perceived as a simple question.

Our mirrors will probably never be spotless in this lifetime. We're in a continual process of healing our perceptions. However, the clearer they are, the more helpful they are. Not only do mirrors reveal our faults, they also reflect our beauty. Most yoga classes end with the greeting, "Namaste," which means, "The light in me sees the light in you." We can recognize the good, the light, the beauty in each other. We can reflect that to one another, just as we can see each other's faults. A good mirror does both.

I wish I had been a better mirror for Luke, able to clearly reflect his own light back to him.

Stewardship, or "Waste Not, Want Not"

Adopting children was very much in line with both my husband's and my practical desire to be good stewards, which probably comes from the (stingy?) Dutch heritage we share. We knew we wanted four children, and it seemed silly to produce all those human beings ourselves when there were so many children already existing in the world who needed families. So we decided on a balanced approach of having two biological children and two adopted. I believe I'm being authentic when I say that D and I did not have grandiose dreams of "rescuing" our adopted children from their impoverished country, like some Superman White Saviors swooping in to save the day. It was really more of a practical decision, it seemed to make sense, and we looked forward to enriching our family and lives through the adventure of cross-cultural adoption.

Wasted resources, especially my own, is a trigger for me. I hate it when I show up to volunteer and end up sitting around because there wasn't enough work or too many volunteers. I hate investing a lot of time and energy cooking a meal only to have it greeted with complaints from picky palates or a nonchalant, "Oh, I already ate!" Having a camper van parked in our yard unused during the winter makes me feel uncomfortable, makes me want to sell it and invest the money or use it to help support our kids.

Luke was an expert at pushing my "don't waste my resources" button. We spent a lot of money and I spent countless hours ferrying Luke around to a plethora of activities, trying to find things that would keep him engaged and happy. Besides the assumed piano lessons and church activities, there were karate lessons, various sports teams, various therapists (mostly Luke's and sometimes our own), summer camps, and numerous friends' homes and activities (Luke had a lot of friends). I invested a lot of time and energy in Luke. And almost invariably a program that we would have Luke enrolled in would come to a premature end. Either Luke would self-sabotage, suddenly deciding that _____ sucked, or his less-than-desirable behaviors would cut the experience short. With each "failed" experience my frustration level increased. As each new endeavor "failed" my subconscious gave me the message that I had failed as a mom. Why was I running around trying this, trying that, when nothing seemed to stick? I felt like Luke was wasting my resources. I was exhausted. And angry.

The visceral response of most people, when they hear of the suicide of a young person, is to say or think, "What a waste!" So much potential, so many life experiences, cut short. To some it appears especially tragic in our situation. Here's Luke—he survived being born to an impoverished single mother in Haiti, survived severe malnourishment as an infant, survived a year plus in an orphanage, survived being uprooted and transplanted into our family in the US, was exceptionally smart, naturally athletic, irresistibly charming to many, a hard worker, managed to graduate high school in the middle of Covid, had a wonderfully supportive girlfriend… a life demonstrating so much resilience and promise. And yet cut short.

I have since come to acknowledge that just because an experience isn't "completed"—just because Luke never went for his black belt, or only did one season with a team, or decided he didn't like a therapist, or broke off a friendship—that doesn't mean that experience was not worthwhile, not worth his effort or my support. Honestly, I'm still struggling to apply this concept to my incomplete LCSW degree. I invested so much money, time, and effort into my education to have it all drop off the side of a cliff, or so it feels. And yet I know, through my whole MSW experience, that I grew and contributed in ways I could not have without it. "Completion" does not equal success. There's value in however long the experience lasts. In fact, sometimes the briefest experiences have the most enduring impact.

Luke's was a life worth living. I will never regret the time, energy, and resources we invested in him. I do regret my attitude at the time. But I was doing the best I knew how. I don't spend a lot of time dwelling on what could have been: What if we could've had more years with Luke to continue improving our relationship— what would that have looked like 5 or 10 years down the road? What could Luke have become—a Starbucks owner? An entrepreneur? A beloved elementary or high school teacher? What if Luke could've married and had children? (We always thought he'd be the one most likely to give us grandchildren.) Instead, I'm grateful for the experience, hard as it was, that we did have with Luke. Grateful for the glimpse of brighter days and restored relationships that we were granted before Luke died. Grateful for the memories of his bright smile and his infectious energy. Grateful for the lessons he continues to teach me. And grateful for the growing conviction that our relationship can and does continue from the other side in a new and discoverable way.

Harvesting Pistachios

A couple years ago D and I took our campervan to New Mexico and happened across "Pistachio Land." Turns out that in the 1980s, a Mr. McGinn had a dream to build a pistachio farm in the desert land of NM. He imported pistachio trees from the Middle East and, through some trial and error, established a prosperous farm which has grown into a well-known roadside attraction selling the best pistachio ice cream I have ever tasted. D and I were able to take a tour of the farm in one of Pistachio Land's extended golf carts.

We learned a lot of interesting facts about pistachio trees that day (for example, they are pollinated by wind, not bees, and just one male tree can pollinate up to thirty female trees). However, what stuck with me most was the explanation of how they harvest the pistachios. There is a machine that grabs hold of the slender trunk of the tree and shakes it forcefully until the nuts, which are actually seeds of fruits, fall off.

Trauma can function like that seemingly heartless harvesting machine. I suppose the machine *is* heartless and has to be to get the job done. Sudden trauma, like Luke's passing, feels like a shaking, a violent shaking. You feel powerless in its grip as it strips you bare. Covid, tsunamis, floods, and fires are that same kind of trauma. As I write this, we're experiencing political trauma in the US. Many, even around the world, are dumbstruck by what's happening. And deeply shaken.

Luke's death, like his life, was a wake-up call for me. However, I didn't quite get it while he was on this earth. Our life together shook me on many levels. However, Luke's death shook me to the core. It forced me to quickly let go of beliefs and attitudes and ideas that I had held onto for 50+ years. It sped up the rate at which I was being transformed. I no longer had the patience for a slow process. I had to change in order to assimilate this tragedy, this new reality. No more pat answers or theoretical beliefs that didn't have practical value to help me through this.

So fitting, for this analogy, that the pistachio nut is actually the seed of a fruit. And that we eat it to nourish our bodies with all the energy of potential that a seed carries. The shaking, and the processing and integrating that follows, often produces seeds: potential for new perspectives, new situations, new service. If we can get to a place of receiving the shaking, it has the potential of releasing fruit beyond our understanding.

LESSON SIX

Rising Above Our Stories

In this life experience we are embedded in stories: stories people tell us and stories we tell ourselves. External stories about what's going on in our world ("The world's going to hell in a handbasket," "AI is going to take over," "Politicians are destroying us") and internal stories we tell ourselves about ourselves ("I'm not good enough," "I'm not as important as _____," "I'm not worthy of ____").

Unfortunately, most of the stories we attach ourselves to tend to be negative or pessimistic. It seems like we unconsciously fall into those, whereas we have to make a conscious effort to create and focus on a positive story. This is true on a societal level (just watch the news) and on an individual level. I've certainly witnessed that same dynamic in the stories I played out with Luke.

My "I am a Victim" Story

I often felt victimized as Luke's mom. I felt like I was Luke's emotional punching bag, taking all the hits for the angst he was experiencing. Starting in late elementary school/early middle school, Luke would yell, scream, punch walls, slam doors, run away, look for support anywhere but at home, and reject anything we would suggest or provide. In fact, our home and family seemed to be a source of acute aggravation to Luke, like nails on a chalkboard constantly sounding in his ears. I felt I bore the brunt of Luke's emotional pain while being absolutely powerless to help him. Both D and I felt like we were living in hell. No doubt Luke did too. I felt like a victim in my own home.

This victimhood mentality was not new for me. I had grown up feeling powerless over my circumstances. When I was 7 years old, my parents divorced, my mom won custody over me and my sister, and we moved hundreds of miles away from my dad whom I loved and was my source of stability. We would see him only periodically from that time forward. In exchange, we were forced to live with my new stepfather who was abusive. Years later I discovered that he sexually abused his first wife, which led her to flee to Europe. Eventually he would also become physically abusive towards my mother which would lead to their divorce. Although I don't remember my stepfather overtly sexually or physically abusing me, he would do sinister things like standing in a doorway so that I'd have to squeeze next to him in order to get through. My stepfather was moody and unpredictable and intimidating. Much like my son Luke would become. It was the perfect set-up for my own emotional triggers and unhealed parts to come bursting through.

And burst through they did. Luke's behaviors triggered an anger in me that I didn't believe I possessed. In fact, at times I almost felt possessed. Like Luke, I would also yell, my body would shake, and I would cry. Luke would punch walls and run; I got a YMCA membership and swam and yoga-ed out that primordial energy that needed to be soothed and released.

I am not proud of the parent I was in those years. At times I found myself almost as dysregulated as Luke. We were like two wild animals caught in a cage, circling each other warily, sometimes taking an offensive swing but mostly fixed in a constant, tense, unpredictable stalemate of a battle. Neither of us seemed to know how to break out of it.

So, feeling useless and victimized at home, I went off to study for my Master of Social Work degree, on a mission to help others when I couldn't help myself. While researching for a paper on Safe Harbor Laws for sex trafficking survivors, I ran across a paper by G. It turns out that G was opening a trauma-informed residential program for female adolescent survivors of sex trafficking in Denver. I'd always felt drawn to serve this population and, spurred by G's passion and in-depth knowledge in this area, I joined her as an intern and later as a paid staff at her residential facility. As part of our on-going training as staff, we were encouraged to participate in mindfulness activities and other therapeutic practices with one of our senior staff, A. During a session with A, as I was complaining about my challenges with Luke and explaining how I felt like a victim in my own home, A asked, "Does that remind you of any situation in your childhood?" It was like a lightbulb went on. I knew then that I was replaying the patterned victim role that I had learned with my stepfather now with Luke. It was automatic for me, when faced with those same kinds of intimidating behaviors, to slip into victim mode. I hadn't learned how to respond any differently. I had never claimed my own power in that kind of a situation. Ironic (or maybe it was the Universe trying to message me) that I was working with these young women, these survivors of sexual abuse, encouraging them to reclaim their personal power, to start new lives, to break out of victimizing patterns, while I was caught in one myself.

Even though it was very dysfunctional, it was my unconscious comfort zone to play the victim, even with my son. Once I recognized where that came from (thank you, A), I could separate it from myself: "Ah, that's a patterned role I learned, it's not who I am!" I realized I had the power to think differently about this situation. I had to let go of the idea, or story, that I was the victim.

Once I could think differently, I could do something different. I could, as the parent—as the change-agent rather than the victim—invite Luke and I out of that cage we were caught in and claim back our relationship.

Following the Wisdom Within

Following our intuition, or the wisdom within, helps us to let go of old stories. Some call it "going with your gut"—trusting your own inner guidance. You might seek the advice of a doctor, or consider the claims of a political party, or confide in a priest, but ultimately you decide if the paths these "experts" lay out for you are a fit for you. That's using your intuition.

In western Christian culture we've developed the habit of giving our power away. We tend to lean on something outside of ourselves to save or guide or lead us. We have not typically been taught to go inside to access our own wisdom, to follow our own path, to tap into the guidance that's uniquely ours. Some of us don't really believe we possess those inner resources, much less the authority to access and act on them. Somehow it's much easier to trust someone outside ourselves to tell us what to do. That's the paradigm we've been raised in.

The reality is that we are each the experts of our own experience. What other human knows us as deeply as we know ourselves? Who can? Each of us is different. Our bodies are different: a medicine that works for one biochemical system may not work for another. Our perspectives are different: one sees the glass half-empty, the other the glass half-full. We have different histories, cultures, and family backgrounds. We've experienced different traumas and joys that have shaped us along the way. What is right for me may not be right for you. Rarely does "one size fit all."

Luke definitely taught us that one style of parenting does not fit all. Methods that were successful with our other children were not with him. And so we ran all around, looking for activities, therapies, schools, and camps to try to help him, and us. At that time I had no idea how to sit still with myself and find higher wisdom. I did pray a lot. And others prayed for us too. We were constantly running around looking for answers outside of ourselves.

I remember two specific times when what I had been taught or told by professionals didn't sit right with me in dealing with Luke's challenging behaviors. As I've mentioned earlier, homework was always a battle with Luke. He just didn't see the point of it or couldn't be bothered. However, my parenting mantra was always, "Homework first—after that, privileges." In high school Luke was recommended by his teachers to be part of an interracial student round-table council, the purpose being to provide feedback and promote more understanding between students and staff/faculty. It was a privilege and wonderful opportunity to be on this council. One particular week Luke had a paper due, in fact, probably over-due. The round-table council meeting was set for a Thursday night, and this paper was due on Friday. Luke came and asked me for a ride to the meeting. I asked him if his paper was done. He said no. I said, "Then I am not going to give you a ride." In response, Luke blew up and slammed a door in my face. That shook me. Then he figured out a bus route and got himself to the meeting.

This was one of many similar incidents, where I/we thought we were doing the normal, logical, consequences/rewards type of parenting and it blew up in our faces. Most of the time I was left feeling bewildered, a bit rattled, but not blown off track. However, this particular time I felt I had missed something, like maybe I needed to go off track, off regular programming. I should have given Luke the ride. In that moment, in those circumstances, the highest good was to give Luke the opportunity to be part of that council, to support him in this unique privilege. That's what my heart wanted to do. But I overruled my heart to follow the system I had created: "Homework first." What was ultimately more important? Acknowledging and supporting my son in this unique and honorable opportunity for service, or guarding the homework rules? I felt I had shut off my internal guidance to follow an external, self-imposed rule.

The other specific time I remember was receiving advice from a therapist. After much searching, we had found a black, male therapist who specialized in adoption/attachment issues. Additional perk: his office was in our neighborhood! Luke, a high school sophomore at the time, saw him twice, I think, and then decided he didn't like him and refused to go back. D and I were also to meet with this therapist, which we were eager to do, hoping he could offer a unique and culturally relevant perspective on our situation. He suggested we create a contract for Luke, spelling out in writing what Luke could expect from us and, in return, what we expected from him, along with consequences if expectations were not met. At first, this sounded like a good idea and we got to work carefully devising the document. I was happy with what we came up with. However, when we thought about actually presenting the document to Luke, it just didn't feel right. It felt like all the old stuff we had already tried and tried with no success. More of the behavior-consequences approach. In the end we scrapped the contract and decided to take Luke out for lunch instead. This time I followed my heart/my intuition instead of the advice from the expert. Granted, that advice may have worked for another child in another family in another situation, but we knew it wasn't right for us. Turns out that lunch was a pivotal event in starting to improve our relationship with Luke.

We can choose who to listen to. We can decide what's right for us. We all have that still, small voice inside, that inner wisdom, that light of God that's uniquely ours that we can tap into. That's our ultimate guidance system, and it may lead us in directions that are not conventional.

Choosing the Meaning of our Stories

Stories are the meaning we put on our experience. We choose that meaning.

The Dalai Lama said that pain is inevitable, suffering is not. I'm still very much trying to grasp this concept. How do we experience pain without suffering?

There's a strong temptation, when your child dies, to stay in grief. I suppose that's true when anyone close to us dies. Of course we need to grieve. We need to acknowledge our losses and pain and feel all the emotions—anger, guilt, despair, numbness, all of it. We need to authentically move through the experience. And the amount of time that takes is different for everyone. But sometimes we don't want to move through our grief. We want to hold on to it. Unconsciously we *choose* to hold on to our grief. Holding on to our grief can feel like honoring our loved one who's passed. *As*

long as I'm sad, I'm acknowledging that person, to myself and to every-
one around me. Letting go of grief feels like letting go of my loved one.
And I will never do that. And so we choose to stay in our grief, in
our suffering.

It took me almost two years to let go of Luke after he died. The
turning point came for me on June 16, 2023 through a healing
session I had with Benny R Ferguson Jr. Before Benny led me in
meditation he asked me what my intentions for the session were.
Generally, I wanted to be released from the constant heaviness I
felt around me since Luke died. Benny mentioned that we've
been conditioned to feel heavy around death but that God/Source
sees death merely as a transition. He then guided me through a
series of visualizations, encouraging me to observe what was
around me in each new scenario that presented itself, and asking
pertinent questions about what I was seeing.

At one point he asked me to shine the light into the idea of the
loss of Luke, into that sadness. As I did so, in my mind's eye I saw
flowers growing (which in this case, Benny said, represented the
transformation of feelings/ideas). Then I saw Luke shooting off
like a firecracker, freed. I immediately felt even more sadness and
grief and started weeping. I was instructed to clear the energies in
the protective sphere I had created at the beginning of our meditation. Then Benny asked me to describe what my grief looked
like in the sphere. I saw a big iron weight set on a pedestal with a
heavy chain attached to it. After asking me about the origin of the
chain, Benny interjected with, "This is a personal endeavor, of
perspective, personal empowerment, change the ideas within
you, that's all you're dealing with." As we probed the scene further, I realized I had a key in my hand, and that the chain was
around my ankle. With Benny's encouragement, I discovered I

could use the key to unlock the chain, which I did. Eventually we went back into the sphere and Benny asked, "Any changes to the block on the stand?" Yes, the block had gotten smaller and smaller, and in its place appeared a horn of plenty! Abundance had replaced heaviness. I wept again, but now with gratitude, feeling relief and hope. Benny concluded with, "You are freer now to become clear, to allow in information for inspiration and be action-oriented toward it." The evidence of that healing is that now, almost two years later, I am finishing my first draft of this book.

It seems, in this life, that we are mostly in the grip of external circumstances, that the things that cause us pain are beyond our control. Our thoughts cannot change the path of a hurricane, for example, or eradicate poverty, or prevent our child from dying. Tragedies are going to happen—they are a part of our human experience. However, I'm slowly learning that my *thoughts* about what happens can lead me on a path of suffering or a path of transformation. I can choose how I want to think about anything that happens. Has Luke come to a tragic end? Or a glorious new beginning? Maybe both. Am I destined to live the rest of my days in grief? Or can I come up with creative ways to continue to honor Luke and his legacy? What do I choose to see on the pedestal life offers me: an iron weight or a horn of plenty?

Ultimately, we have the power to choose the meaning we attach to our experiences. And it's probably the only real power we have.

Othello (the game), or "Dueling with Duality"

I've always enjoyed playing games with my kids. One game we would often play (and in fact is still in our game cupboard) is called Othello, a 2-person game played with 2-sided discs about the size of quarters. One side of the disc is white, the other black. Players take turns placing their discs on a grid that looks like a chess board. Each player tries to "capture" their opponent's color by placing his own color on both ends of an opposite-colored row of discs. Each time a player manages to do that, he can flip all the in-between discs to his own color. The person who has the most of his color on the board by the time all the squares are filled wins.

The game of Othello can serve as an analogy for the way we think. Mostly we think in terms of black and white, good and bad, harmful and helpful. Some call that "dualistic" thinking, "dual" referring to only two options being available. This kind of thinking is very helpful for basic survival, which requires us to quickly judge, for example, if the tiger coming toward us is "good" or "bad" and take action accordingly. On one level, we need to categorize our experiences in order to survive.

We can also think of black and white as two sides of the same coin, or disc in terms of Othello. The disc *appears* to be black when the black side is flipped up, and white when the white side is flipped up. However, everyone knows that the disc is always both black and white—the other color is just on the unflipped side. Recognizing that two opposites are part of the same whole is called "non-dualistic" thinking. It's thinking beyond black and white, good and bad, harmful and helpful. It's accepting that what we might judge as "bad" can, in the overall picture, be "good." And vice-versa. It just depends how the disc is flipped in any particular moment.

Flipping the disc can represent changing our perspective. We have the power to flip the disc. We can choose how to think about any experience or situation in our lives. We can rise above our stories by choosing a larger perspective, one that does not hold us captive to our good/bad categories.

This is a challenge, to say the least. Some things are clearly bad: abuse, natural disasters, disease, suicide, to name a few. This life is not a game where we can simply flip awful experiences into good ones.

The key, I think, is to know that the bad/evil is part of a greater whole. We may not be able to see the good, but we believe it's there, even while we experience the pain and suffering. I experienced good-in-bad in all the love and support and synchronicities that happened around Luke's memorial, that "terrible, awe-full" time. I also think of the recent devastating fires in California. People there repeatedly reported that "in the worst of times, the best of humanity comes out": neighbors who lost their houses helped others save theirs, numerous restaurants donated time and labor and food to set up free dining areas for rescue workers, and people across the nation prayed. Historically, I also think of those Holocaust survivors who were miraculously able to survive the atrocities of the camps by maintaining hope of rescue, persevering in their belief that there was a larger reality than what they were currently suffering.

I never fully grasped, until I Googled it just now, why the game Othello was named Othello. As you might have guessed, the creator named it after the Shakespeare tragedy. In the play, Othello, a person of color, is deceived by his angry, non-approving white father-in-law into thinking that his wife, Desdemona, a white woman, has been cheating on him. In a rage, Othello murders his wife. After realizing he had been deceived and mistaken, Othello kills himself.

The play Othello demonstrates the power of deception. And, I would add, perception. How fitting for our analogy. The great deception is that there is no good in the bad, or bad in the good. It's actually vital for our survival to see the bigger picture, to be able to see the good-in-bad (and sometimes the bad-in-good), to maintain the belief that there is a larger whole, a larger story, that is holding everything together. Trusting in the bigger story can give us the courage and strength to flip our perspective, if we so choose.

What If We Are the Creators of Our Stories?

In the years since Luke passed, I've learned about something called "soul planning." It's a big concept, and sometimes hard to swallow. Soul planning asserts that on some level, on our soul-level, we've planned everything we're experiencing, the good and the bad. The idea is that we've *chosen* what we're experiencing, that *we've* chosen what we're experiencing.

I grew up with the assurance that no matter what happens in our lives, God has a plan. Soul planning comes out of that same kind of assumption, only the plan is not conceived by some Force outside of ourselves but by our own eternal soul (God-within-us) in conjunction with other eternal souls. We decide what we want to learn or experience in any given lifetime—challenges and pain as well as triumphs and joy—for the common purpose of growth and expansion.

Soul planning is the idea that each of us, as an eternal soul, plans our lives in cooperation with other souls. It's not a plan filled with details or fixed in stone since all the players have free will and that can lead to endless possibilities about how the plan will be worked out. Basically, the plan centers around experiences (some call it lessons) our souls want to experience (or learn) during a lifetime, all for the purpose of mutual growth and expansion.

We all agree to take on certain roles for the benefit of all. For example, one soul may decide to have a physical disability in this life, perhaps to experience what that limitation feels like for themselves, and to provide another soul with the experience of caretaking. The caretaking soul may want to develop compassion, empathy, and patience in this life, and so the two souls come up with this plan together. Expand this scenario unlimited times to encompass all the players and all the experiences that could be gleaned from this central plot.

Soul planning assumes reincarnation. That is, as souls, we can incarnate multiple times and have unlimited experiences. The possibilities are endless. The learning and expanding are infinite. The world becomes our playground, our canvas, our mountain of fresh powder-snow to play and create and adventure in.

One author (I wish I could remember who it was) suggested that God/Source split himself into an infinite number of pieces, a little bit of him in each and every thing he created, in order to grow and develop and expand himself. Just as we live and breathe and move in him, he lives and breathes and moves in us. We're all in this journey of expansion together, in a beautiful flow of discovery. In this model, there is no "God" and "us" as separate entities, one dictating The Plan to the other. We are free to create and explore for the benefit of all, with the ever-present support of God or Source, who delights in whatever adventure we choose.

Soul planning is a concept that has been developed by authors such as Brian Weiss in *Many Lives, Many Masters*, Michael Newton in *Journey of Souls*, Christian Sundberg in *A Walk in the Physical*, and Robert Schwartz in *Your Soul's Plan*. Through their work facilitating past-lives regression therapy and/or through personal experience, these authors have proposed that we, as souls, have planned our lives—that we have literally created our own stories.

Luke's Story

Within the framework of this idea of soul planning, I can just imagine Luke's soul stepping up to the plate, asking for a triple portion of everything this life could offer him! That would be so fitting of his character as I knew him. Luke was a go-getter, full of energy, hard-working, always looking for the next activity, be that physical, mental or social. And he seemed equipped to take it all on, being naturally street smart, book smart, physically fit, and skilled in multiple arenas.

If you've read all the pages before this, you have a pretty good idea of what Luke said yes to:

"Yes! I'll be born in the impoverished, conflict-ridden country of Haiti."

"Yes! I'll be born to a single, poor, unsupported mother in Port-au-Prince."

"Yes! I'll almost die as an infant due to malnutrition."

"Yes! I'll spend my most formative first two years in a hospital and orphanage."

"Yes! I'll be whisked away by strangers to live in a foreign country with a language, food, and culture completely unfamiliar to me."

"Yes! I'll grow up in a mostly white family as their black son and have parents who (at least at the beginning) are largely ignorant of everything that will affect me."

"Yes! I'll grow up in the social fabric of the United States which is mostly antagonistic to young black men."

"Yes! I'll be exceptionally smart and sensitive so that everything impacts me to the max."

"Yes! I'll struggle with depression/anger/suicidal thoughts most of my life."

Why would a soul like Luke sign up for all of that? I don't pretend to know completely. However, I do have hunches, based on who I knew him to be.

For one, as previously alluded to, *Luke was always one to take on a challenge.* He enjoyed pushing himself to the limit. He was always wanting to learn something new.

Secondly, *Luke had a desire to serve.* When Luke was in elementary school, he and I went to the aviation museum, just to do something fun together (a rare happening with four kids at home). As we were wandering around looking at the life-sized plane models, we ended up next to a person who needed help of some kind. I can't remember specifically what kind of help. What I do remember is that, before I knew it, Luke had run off to get what that person needed. It was a moment etched into my memory because I felt like Luke was acting out of his best self, totally unguarded, following his heart—something he rarely seemed able to do.

Luke proved to be stellar at fast-food service, first at Chick-fil-A and then at Starbucks. He was fast and had the uncanny ability to be aware of many things at once. And he was (mostly) glad to serve people. Often he went out of his way to do so, as we learned from the man, R, who helped us purchase Luke's memorial boulder. Turns out R worked with a woman at the mortuary who regularly frequented the Starbucks where Luke worked. R was eager to share that when his coworker heard about Luke's death, she broke down and cried. Turns out Luke had repeatedly gone above and beyond in serving her coffee—bringing it out to her car in bad weather, for example—and always greeted her with his warm and winning smile. It seems Luke had made a lasting impression, even through those brief interactions.

97

When he was in a good head space, Luke would voluntarily help with household chores, like shoveling snow or helping D build a chicken coop. He liked to make waffles for our family. Generally, he liked to be active and involved and contribute.

So I have a hunch Luke signed up for the life he did for the purpose of serving those around him. I know he was a light to many while he was on this earth. Many experienced him as the kind, generous, empathetic person he was. Some of us also experienced his darker side, especially those of us who lived with him. Luke brought many challenges into our lives, through his life and through his death. Challenges that had and have the potential to transform us. At this point, almost four years after Luke's death, I can witness transformation in myself—ways I've expanded that I probably would not have without Luke in my life. This book is a testimony to that.

Victims or Warriors?

Does life happen to us, or do we happen to life? Are we victims of our circumstances or warriors of our experience? (This is a concept I learned about through Tara Arnold.)

I'm still wrapping my head around the idea that we can be, or are, warriors of our experience. Soul planning assumes that we actually choose the experiences of our lives, that we volunteer for our challenges. On a higher level, our souls understand that the difficulties we live with here on earth have a greater purpose: to expand us in ways we could not otherwise expand. We need the light *and* the dark to grow as humanity. Our ultimate challenge is to learn to receive both good and bad with an open hand.

It helps me to think that God/Source/the-Benevolence-holding-our-universe-together works with our own higher selves or souls to come up with the plan for our lives. The plan is not a thing forced on us without our permission—it's a cooperative venture, decided for the common highest good and divine purpose. There is a bigger picture that my finite intellect cannot always understand. But my soul—that spark of God within me, that eternal presence—does.

I think Luke bit off more than he could chew. All the challenges his soul signed up for in this life proved to be too much. That's one perspective I could take. And/or maybe suicide was part of the plan—one body broken for the expansion of many; Luke continuing to challenge and shift our perspectives in death as he did in life. Challenging us to look beyond our categories of good and bad, black and white. Challenging us to open to a larger perspective, one that enables us to receive everything offered (chosen) in this cornucopia of life, trusting that it's all working together for the benefit of all.

Going With the Flow

"Flow," "follow," "allow"—all these words seem related. What's the wisdom here? To flow, to follow, to allow—all contain the word "low." There's something about going low that allows us to flow.

It's easy to get swept up in the current of fear and despair during times of chaos and confusion. Or, we might get angry and try to swim against the current, which may offer some hope in the short-term but is rarely sustainable. So how do we maintain our balance and any sense of peace when our world is in turmoil?

We go deeper. We go low. Rather than rising above the chaos, we go through it to what's below.

99

We anchor ourselves in bedrock truths that will outlast whatever chaos is on the surface.

What are some of those bedrock truths? Consider these:

- There is a greater Flow which requires a process, sometimes even a battle, to be played out. "All great changes are preceded by chaos" (Deepak Chopra).

- What we see around us is temporary. It's not fixed, it's constantly changing, like the surface of the water. "This too shall pass."

- Peace is the greater reality. It's the still point of the swinging pendulum, that resting point that the wild extremes always return to. Peace is the universe's homeostasis: an internal programming back to balance. "Peace I leave with you; my peace I give to you" (Jesus, John 14:27).

Anchoring ourselves in truths like these does not automatically make the current of chaos disappear. But it helps us not get swept away by it. We "stay" ourselves; we remain in a calm state or condition. The more we as individuals are able to remain in that state, and the more of us collectively remain in that state, the more influence we have on the chaos around us. We become stabilizers that the rest of reality adjusts to.

In psychology, this is called co-regulation, and I learned it's key when caring for traumatized children. When a child is having a tantrum, the best (and probably the hardest) thing you can do is remain calm. Your internal harmony will eventually (and it may take hours) cause the child's dysregulated system to fall in sync. This is what a soothing parent does for a crying baby. It's what a therapy animal does for an anxious patient. There is amazing healing power in moving through our worlds in a consistently regulated state.

I wish I could say I did that for Luke: that I was that consistent peaceful, regulating presence in his life. I was not. Many times my dysregulation almost matched his. My dear friend, S, would always remind me that "this too shall pass," but it felt, at the time, that the challenging times with Luke would never end. I often got swept up in the chaos. I definitely felt unanchored—not knowing, or maybe forgetting, what I could hold on to. Honestly, sometimes I didn't feel like holding on to anything. I was exhausted and preferred that the current just take me where it willed, or that I got out of the river altogether.

These are the bedrock truths that remain, that were always there, and that found me again—these are what I hold on to:

- Luke is my loved and chosen son.
- Beneath our often chaotic relationship, there was always love.
- That love endures, even after death.

LESSON SEVEN

It's Okay to Die

When you're 19 years old and suffering within and without, it's okay to die.

When you're a baby in the womb and your life is not viable, it's okay to die.

When you're a child with terminal cancer, it's okay to die.

When you're a person in a fatal car accident, it's okay to die.

When you're a middle-aged person gravely sick with Covid, it's okay to die.

When you're 90 and have lived a full life, it's okay to die.

Most of us have no problem with that last statement. Yes, it's okay to die when you're 90. The previous statements can make our hearts, our minds, even our bodies viscerally react with, "No, that is NOT okay!" Those statements may sound heretical and hurtful, especially to those of us who have experienced loved ones passing in those ways.

Of course, I am not condoning suicide or cancer or car accidents or Covid, as if we should simply accept all the things that cause us suffering. However, young or old, by accident or disease (physical or mental), at our own hand or at the hand of another, death is inevitable. It is our common fate. But somehow we persist in resisting it. I've come to believe that our resistance to death has a lot to do with our beliefs about it.

Death as the Enemy

Being born in the double-doozy of both western and Christian culture, I grew up with the message that death is the enemy. There are passages in the Bible, like 1 Corinthians 15, that describe death as "the last enemy to be destroyed." The hymns we sang every Sunday in church regularly included proclamations that Jesus has conquered death. That's the whole point of Easter, after all. Added to that is western culture's pervasive and seemingly endless preoccupation with staying young. Old age is not honored; in fact, it's kind of embarrassing to get older. Often wrinkles and belly fat come paired with a natural demotion in social status. We don't talk about our path toward death. We generally try to avoid the subject.

Whoever made death the enemy? Why are we so afraid of death, personifying it as the Grim Reaper and associating it with the devil? At best, we run away from death, and if we can't run away, we feel compelled to destroy or conquer it in some way. Sometimes death is even seen as kind of a moral failure. We have to fight death, and if we don't—for example, if we decide against a life-saving procedure, or make our own plan for how we will die—we are judged, maybe even put in jail. Sometimes, at all costs, we are mandated to preserve life and resist death.

Death as a Robber

When someone dies young, we often say they "died before their time." But who's setting the schedule? Really, it's the expectations of the ones they left behind. We don't expect or want anyone to die young. However, that doesn't mean it was not their time. Obviously, it was their time. But not ours.

The death of our loved ones is so painful because *our* time with them was cut short. We can't hug them anymore, or cook them dinner, or perhaps seize all the moments to say "sorry" and "I love you" that we wish we would have done when they were with us. They're gone. We even sometimes say, when someone dies, that "God has taken" that person from us. Taken our future together. Taken all the life-events we looked forward to experiencing together: holidays, weddings, even the simple day-to-day. Bottom line: death steals what's ours, or what we thought was ours.

Death as the Unknown

What happens when we die? There doesn't seem to be a lot of consensus about that. Some of us believe our loved ones simply cease to exist. Some of us believe in hell and eternal damnation. Others believe there is a heaven and our loved ones are there, but heaven is mysterious and its inhabitants largely unreachable.

Several years before Luke died, I attended a Richard Rohr conference in Albuquerque, New Mexico. Father Richard was giving away (actually selling very cheaply for charity) many books from his personal library. One in particular intrigued me: *The Journey Home: What Near-Death Experiences and Mysticism Teach Us About the Gift of Life* by Phillip L. Berman. After Luke died, I listened to and read many more accounts of Near Death Experiences, or NDEs. (If you want to do the same, Anita Moorjani's *Dying to Be Me* may be a place to start.) Most NDE-ers describe going to "the other side" as coming home in a way they've never experienced before. They consistently describe being greeted by an overwhelming sense of love from God or Source, and from the presence of passed loved ones, angels, and guides. Many of them say the other side felt more like their home than anything else ever had. At the same time, the colors and sounds, the beauty and depth of the experience, was beyond their imagination and hard to put into words. Many of them do not want to return to their earthly lives but do so because of uncompleted missions here. They come back with a deep conviction of what their earthly purpose is and a passion to fulfill it, enabled by the incredible heavenly love they now know is supporting them.

Experiencing Luke's Death

Admittedly, Luke's death has deeply influenced the way I now perceive death in general.

For one thing, death is not shocking to me anymore. It's not sensational or scary. I've been largely desensitized to it. A couple of years after Luke died, I had the privilege of leading a grief group for kids at Montessori del Mundo elementary school. I actually looked forward to it. I felt a kinship with these children who were also grieving. I had a deep desire to normalize death and grief for them.

I no longer view death as the enemy, as something to be resisted. I actually found it odd, observing myself after Luke died, that I had no desire to go out and speak against suicide or start a suicide prevention campaign, as many others do after experiencing such a loss. Please know that I am not condoning suicide in any way. The act that seemingly ends pain for one brings pain for many others. However, for myself as Luke's mom, I know that, at that moment, death brought Luke relief when nothing else could. And, as I stated in my eulogy, his decision to take his life was probably the one thing he had ever had complete control of. Luke spent his life tossed around by both the chaos in his head and the chaos without, being completely uprooted from his original environment and then living as a young black man in America and as a black adopted child in a mostly white family. There was precious little peace to be had in a life like his. He faced a plethora of challenges within and without. I don't judge him for choosing eternal peace. Sometimes death is mercy.

I'm coming to accept that death is not a robber but part of the process, even when it comes at a time we don't expect. Death is part of the fabric in which we live. It's the nature of our environment. It's a necessary part of the process here on earth. Every fall, things die. Every spring, they come back to life. Then the next fall they die again, and come up again in the spring. True, some things don't come back again. But then their decaying bodies provide nourishment for some other form of life. Death is a necessary part of the recycling program. Death is not an aberration, a departure from what's normal. Death *is* normal; it's normal to die.

For me, the "other side" is becoming less mysterious, as it seems to be for a lot of people. There are now organizations such as IANDS, the International Association for Near Death Studies, established in the USA in 1981, for the purpose of studying and sharing information about NDEs. And academics such as Dr. Gary Schwartz from the Department of Neurology at the University of Arizona who is developing instruments to measure the presence of those who have passed on and now exist in spirit form. In 2024 D and I attended the Helping Parents Heal conference in Arizona where over 1000 parents whose children have died gathered with NDE experiencers, mediums, and researchers to learn more about the afterlife and how to connect with their children. What was once considered taboo is slowly becoming mainstream. What was once considered unknowable is slowly becoming known.

My own spiritual experiences with Luke, both facilitated by others and experienced on my own, have convinced me that his spirit is still alive and active on the other side. Death is not the final curtain, the ultimate separation. It's a transition to another state, and one that we are learning to access. Death *feels* like a robber. But maybe it's merely a doorman, helping us all return home.

We Are More Than Our Bodies

> *We are not human beings having a spiritual experience; we are spiritual beings having a human experience.*
>
> —*Pierre Teilhard de Chardin*

Never was this made more clear to me than when I saw Luke's broken body laying in the casket. Luke was clearly not there. His essence was somewhere else. His body was just an empty shell. Surely he was more than his body!

If we could acknowledge, while we're living in our bodies, that we are more than our bodies, maybe we would not be so afraid of and repulsed by death. Maybe we would not have to cling so tightly to these temporary tents. Maybe we could recognize and accept the death of our bodies for what is—the end of one experience and the beginning of another. A transformation. A transition. A gateway to something else.

My daughter, L, works as a social worker with seniors. Once an aging man asked her where we go after we die. She replied that we probably return to the same place we came from before we were born. A simple answer, and a wise and comforting one. Yes, we came from somewhere, so it makes sense that we'd be going somewhere too. Intuitively we know this is true. We know we are much more than these physical shells.

The Art of Letting Go, or Getting Used to Dying

We had a butterfly release at Luke's memorial—one of the many things that seemed to fall into our laps and fall into place for that day. There was something so comforting about holding the precious butterfly packet in my hands, having the privilege to open it, providing my steady and still palms as a platform for the butterfly to slowly wake up and adjust, and finally, witnessing its effortless flight to the nearest flower. The butterfly release was a physical representation of what we were all doing that day: letting Luke go. And trusting that there was somehow beauty in the process.

Death forces us to let go, suddenly and dramatically. It feels more like something is being ripped out of our hands than that we are voluntarily letting go, but ultimately, we have to give in to what has happened, to acknowledge it and accept it. We have to release our grip.

Our bodies are constantly doing this, without our conscious permission or consent. Every day, about 330 billion of our human cells are shed and replaced. Every 7 to 10 years *all* the cells in our body are replaced. We're constantly letting things go on the physical level. There's an innate cycle of dying and rebirth that's a necessary process for our growth and development. This is true on a psychological level as well. We need to let things die to make way for the new.

Forgiving is an act of letting go that can feel like a kind of death.

For a lot of us, it's hard to forgive. It feels like we're giving up something that shouldn't be given up: justice. If we hold on to what that person did to us and never forget it, it feels like they're being held accountable. In reality we're just getting eaten up by our own resentment. That other person may not even realize we're upset, may never take accountability for their actions. Forgiveness can feel like a little death, a giving up, a letting go, a releasing. It's hard. But we do it. Sometimes to amazing extremes. Like Immaculee Ilibagiza who survived the Rwandan genocide by hiding in a 3x4-foot bathroom with seven other women for 91 days, and ultimately forgave those who killed her entire family. Or like Louie Zamperini in the film *Unbroken* who forgives the Japanese captors who brutally tortured him as a prisoner of war.

Asking for forgiveness may be even harder than granting it. My time in the 12 Steps taught me something about that. Steps 8 and 9 encourage participants to "Make a list of everyone you've harmed" and "Become willing to make amends to everyone on the list." Making amends means going to the person you've harmed, naming your offence, and sincerely apologizing for your actions (if doing so would not cause further harm to the recipient). At that time, the number one person on my list was my husband. Ouch. Humbling myself to ask his forgiveness was a painful process. Also like a death, a death to self, an acknowledgement that maybe I'm part of the problem.

I'm part of the problem. I, too, need forgiveness. When we get to that point, maybe the hardest process to submit to is *self*-forgiveness: "I screwed up but I'm still worthy, I'm still loveable and able to love." Usually, we're our own worst critic and judge.

I believe the thing that tipped Luke over the edge happened the night before he died. It was his own moral failure that he finally just couldn't live with. He knew he had hurt the person he loved most, and he could not bear that. He did not have the capacity to forgive himself.

Forgiving others, asking others to forgive us, forgiving ourselves—these are little (or big) ways we practice dying little deaths. And sometimes our very lives depend on it.

LESSON EIGHT

It's Okay To Let Go of What We Know

Reflecting back on our years together I can now realize and appreciate that Luke was constantly challenging me to let go of what I thought I knew.

I Thought I Knew How to Parent

We were blissfully ignorant when we adopted Luke. We already had three children by then—H and J, our biological children, and L, our adopted Haitian daughter. None of them challenged us as parents like Luke challenged us. Yes, parenting at its baseline requires sacrifice and commitment and is in that way inherently challenging. However, Luke introduced us to a whole set of behaviors and dispositions that we had never encountered before. We were often at a complete loss as to how to parent him.

Unprepared for Battles

Our other three children responded quite seamlessly to the rules and boundaries we established with them. It's not like we were strict parents (as our kids would report to us after hearing about how their friends' parents ran their households) but we did insist on things like eating supper together, going to church together, doing your homework, etc. Luke would challenge us repeatedly, even on those (what I would consider) basics. Food and eating were a constant issue for him, which we came to understand is quite common for adopted, traumatized children. It made even more sense in the light of Luke's severe malnourishment as an infant. However, understanding where his pickiness and refusal around food came from didn't mean we knew how to handle it, or our own frustration. Mealtimes became battles.

I remember the first time we took Luke to our quite formal, stoic, ritualized church. We wanted to keep him with us rather than subjecting him to yet another unfamiliar environment: that of the church nursery. He made a game out of squirming out of my arms, crawling under the (empty) pew in front of us and back up and over it, back into my arms. In those early days we were enamored and laughed and played along with him (as quietly as we could in that church setting). However, over time the cute toddler behavior was replaced with a sour sullenness at going to church with the family. That, too, became a battle. (However, we are grateful that we later became part of Colorado Community Church, a multi-racial, non-denominational church which had programs for youth that Luke was mostly happy to be a part of.)

School, oh my—probably the biggest battlefield of all. Luke would have gotten into a lot more trouble were it not for his charm and good looks. Seriously. In first grade he was often sent for a time-out for socializing too much and not doing the assigned work. Luke was always a social magnet. I was in awe of how he could somehow sweet talk teachers into excusing him from completing assignments that other students were held accountable for. Homework was a constant battle. He just couldn't be bothered, thought the assignments were stupid and a waste of time. Perhaps they were. However, not completing homework was not in my parenting worldview. I had been a good student, and our three other children were all good students—not all A students, but all did their best. Again, I was stumped as to how to support Luke through school. He was exceptionally smart and exceptionally resistant. Fortunately, for the most part, Luke attended wonderful schools (including highly gifted and talented and accelerated high school programs) with supportive teachers and administrations that saw him through to graduation (even in the middle of Covid), despite the challenges he presented.

The Rules Don't Apply...

Luke behaved in ways that dumbfounded us. And angered us. For me, lying and deceit was a big trigger. When our kids were young, they each had a piggy bank divided into three sections (thank you Dave Ramsey): one for spending, one for saving, and one for giving. Ten percent would go to "giving," twenty percent to saving, and the rest for spending. Every week I would tally up what we owed each child for the chores they'd done and go to the bank for the correct change so they could each put the appropriate percentages in each section of their bank. It was quite the process. Sometimes we would sit together and divvy out the coins but usually I gave each child their money, told them how much for each section, and trusted them to allot it appropriately. No problem for our three oldest. However, Luke caught on that I didn't always monitor their piggy banks, and he would regularly put all the money in his spending section or hide it for spending later. Looking back, I can laugh and even admire Luke for his shrewdness, but it was NOT funny at the time. We went through a lot of effort to teach our kids early how to handle money. Every time Luke lied about his money and disregarded our system, it felt like a personal affront to our parenting. Like he was continually rejecting what we had to offer.

Cell phones were another HUGE issue. We had a rule that our kids could not have a cell phone until their freshman year of high school. Admittedly, that was okay for our older children but became more of a social challenge as cell phones became more rampantly used by the time our younger two got to high school. However, we thought it important to be consistent with the same boundary for all of our kids (was it actually important? I'm not sure). Luke, being the social magnet that he was, *needed* a cell phone by middle school for sure. Somehow, he would convince classmates to give him or buy him cell phones, even participating in their families' phone plans! We had many battles and confiscated numerous phones from Luke. Once we finally conceded and bought him his own phone (*before* his freshman year) the challenge became putting parameters around the use of the phone. We had another rule that everyone put their cell phone in the kitchen before they went to bed at night. Luke often refused. Or he would somehow have another phone hidden that he used at night. Again, looking back, it was rather amazing how Luke maneuvered his way around and through us to get his cell phone needs met. And again, it was NOT amazing at the time. It felt like defiance and like a rejection of the good parenting we were offering him. (So appropriate and amazing that Luke would make his presence known to us after his death in the cell phone shop!)

Another thing I was not prepared for as a parent was anger—Luke's and my own. When we tried to reinforce our parental rules and boundaries, Luke would not object quietly. He would yell, rage, slam doors, punch walls, run away. His angry behavior was always startling and unsettling, and as he became older and bigger it felt increasingly threatening.

Bottom line is, the parenting style we knew was not working with Luke. We felt like we were hitting our heads against a brick wall with him. Seemed like everything was a battle. The more we tried to be consistent, the more intense the battles became.

Our Parenting Isn't Working...

About a year and a half before Luke transitioned, I was in training to be a TBRI Practitioner. TBRI is an abbreviation for Trust-Based Relational Intervention, which is a trauma-informed model of caregiving for those who are parenting or in any way engaged with traumatized children. The TBRI modality is considered somewhat "cutting-edge" and at the same time is a kind of reverting back to a grandmother's wisdom: focusing on the relationship and meeting the underlying needs of the child. In TBRI we are encouraged to see "bad" behavior as communication, to see beyond the behavior to the unmet needs causing it. For example, why does a child lie? TBRI says a child lies because that child doesn't feel safe and doesn't trust that his or her needs are going to be met. Lying is the parents' cue—not to punish, but to reinvest in the relationship with the child and try to understand the underlying (no pun intended!) unmet need.

When I started the TBRI training, the concepts sounded vaguely familiar, like I had heard them before. Only as I got further into it did I realize that D and I had attended a very similar training many years earlier called Connected Parenting. We knew that we needed a new parenting model. However, I think at that time we did not have the bandwidth or maybe even the desire to integrate

121

and implement what we were hearing. We already felt stretched beyond our parenting resources and now we were being asked to do more, to spend more time with Luke, to build a stronger connection with him. It felt like too much. Besides, it felt like Luke was constantly rejecting us and our efforts. He consistently refused to participate in or sabotaged family events. Did he even want a deeper relationship with us? We doubted that.

We spent more time, energy, and money on Luke than any of our other kids. I researched and enrolled Luke in schools with special advanced programs to try to keep his extraordinary intelligence engaged. We switched to a new church that was multiracial and had dynamic kids' programming that Luke could be a part of. We went to Heritage Adoption Camps where Luke could be surrounded by kids who looked like him, in multi-racial families that looked like ours. We took him to Haiti for a "birth land tour" to help Luke develop and take pride in that part of his identity. At that time we offered him a search for his birth mother, but he declined. He was a gifted athlete, and we had him in sports camps, school sports teams, community sports teams, karate lessons. He went to Christian summer camp (which he loved). We tried several therapists (Luke was resistant and didn't like any of them) and participated in family therapy and individual therapy. D and I were both on antidepressants ourselves, and offered that Luke be on them too, to help him deal with his anger and depression. He refused. There were moments of joy and accomplishments, but overall, Luke's general unhappiness persisted. And overall, I felt inadequate as his mother. Nothing I/we tried seemed to work to alleviate Luke's internal pain. To top it off, during this time, Luke would adopt his friends' families and call their moms "mama (insert first name)", and refer to his female friends as his "real" sisters.

That broke my heart. And, to be honest, boiled my blood.

Eventually we/I stopped trying so hard. If Luke wanted distance from us, we'd give him distance. If he wanted absolute freedom and independence, we'd give him that. It felt like we made the decision to abdicate being Luke's parents. Luke had his first job at 14 and was earning his own money so we had him pay for his own cell phone bill in order to eradicate all those battles. We still provided food and lodging but that was about it. It was almost like living as roommates, each of us doing our own thing, interacting only if there was a chance encounter in the kitchen. It felt awful. It felt like self-preservation, and it felt awful. This was definitely not the future we envisioned when we picked up that shy, charming boy, with his disarming smile and resolute spirit, from the orphanage in Port-au-Prince all those years ago. We never imagined that Luke would do anything other than blend seamlessly into our family. To put it succinctly, we didn't know sh**.

A Slow Turn...

Maybe it was the act of letting go as parents, maybe it was the space we had created, maybe it was the unexpected changes that Covid brought, maybe it was the new love Luke found with his committed girlfriend, but somehow things began to become a little smoother for the three of us as Luke approached the end of high school. Being largely confined to home during that March 2020 Covid quarantine in some ways seemed to be a relief to Luke. It was like he could let go of the pressures of keeping up with all the social dynamics and pressures of school (which he had made a full-time job of doing). He seemed more relaxed at home. We ate more meals together and had a few more conversations.

During those months I happened to be reading a book by Lorna

Byrne entitled *A Message of Hope from the Angels*. In it she suggested that when in conflict with a person, take them to a public, neutral place where guards can be down and tempers in check, and just invite a conversation. Her advice resonated with me. It seemed like a new and fresh approach we could take with Luke, and it seemed we were all ready for it. D and I invited Luke to lunch and although the invitation took him by surprise and he was probably somewhat suspicious of our motives, he accepted (who can resist Torchy's Tacos?). We had a pleasant conversation in which Luke shared more than we had ever heard before about his plans and dreams for after high school graduation. We were able to make a plan to support him for his next steps. Deeper than that, we were all able to recognize that beyond the struggle, the baseline truth was that we all cared for each other and wanted to give and receive each other's support. We were family.

We were grateful that in May of 2020, in spite of Covid and many missed assignments throughout the years, Luke graduated. He would spend the next several months living with us at home, working many shifts at various Starbucks, saving money, and basically waiting out Covid and his own indecision about a college path. When Luke had the opportunity, in the spring of 2021, to move out of our home and in with a friend in Boulder, it was a peaceful and cordial transition, for which we were very thankful. We kept in touch after the move, taking Luke out for lunch here and there and having regular text conversations. He would ask me how to cook certain things. Once he baked cookies and delivered some as a surprise to our mailbox! He was perhaps happier and more settled than he ever had been. And we could see that he, indeed, even after all the conflict we experienced in our home, still wanted a relationship with us. I felt like I was slowly getting my son back. Like there was hope for our relationship. I could hug him and feel it reciprocated. We could have genuine conversations. He went out of his way to participate in family activities and was happy to do so. He wanted to share his life with us.

I was both deeply saddened and immensely grateful that my/our relationship with Luke was in a good place when he passed. Saddened, at all the future potential and promise ended so abruptly. Grateful, that I did not have to carry the extra emotional baggage of anger and guilt that I had developed throughout the hellish years of parenting Luke as I experienced the anguishing grief of his death. His final text, just before he took his own life, was to D and I. His last words were, "I love you."

I Thought I Knew What I Believed

A dear Christian friend I've had since childhood recently asked me if Luke's death has shaken my faith. No, Luke's passing has not shaken my faith. It has blown it up. Not blown up as in destroyed, not like Ground Zero, but blown up as in expanded, like filling a huge hot air balloon. But much bigger than that, more like the explosions that create new stars and galaxies. Mind-blowing expansion. An expansion that I'm only beginning to grasp.

Needing More than Platitudes

When I saw Luke's broken body in the casket—hopefully the hardest thing I'll ever have to look at in this lifetime—it was clear he wasn't there. The life force, the spirit, the personality, everything that enlivened that being, was gone. I knew instinctively that Luke still existed. All my life I had ascribed to the belief in eternal life. But what did that really mean for my son and for me right now? Knowing that Luke was "in heaven" wasn't cutting it for me anymore. Where exactly was heaven? Where was Luke? He still existed, but exactly how?

In the weeks and months following Luke's passing, having lost my job and desiring little else but to isolate in the comfort of home, I did a lot of exploring on YouTube. Lorna Byrne was my first search. I had heard of her years before when the CD of her autobiography, *Angels in My Hair*, caught my eye as I perused the library shelves for something to listen to on my long solo drive back from Alabama to Colorado after dropping Luke's older sister off at college. Lorna is an Irish mystic who has seen angels, physically, all her life. Listening to her stories of ministering angels gave me comfort at that time, in the wake of saying goodbye to my daughter. And I needed comfort now more than ever.

As I listened to Lorna being interviewed, I would take comfort in her peaceful presence and in her conviction that there are angels all around us, helping us. I guess I had heard that, in a theoretical way, all my life through my Christian upbringing, but I had never practically believed it—I had never personally called on angels to help me, or even really thought about the possibility. Lorna sees that each of us has a personal guardian angel that is with us throughout our lives, guiding and supporting us along each of our unique paths—with us when we are born and when we die. That message gave me a lot of comfort when I thought of Luke dying alone, without my or any human comfort. Perhaps the white, feathery bird I saw in my dream had been a form of

Luke's guardian angel, supporting and protecting him at the moment of his passing. "Are not all angels ministering spirits sent to serve those who will inherit salvation?" (Hebrews 1:14).

In one Lorna Byrne interview I watched, the interviewee was Helping Parents Heal (HPH), an organization whose mission is just that: to help parents heal from the passing of their children. This was my introduction to HPH and they in turn introduced me to a plethora of other spiritual teachers and seekers who were asking all the big questions: Why are we here? How do we make sense of suffering? How does our world really work? At the same time I listened to and read a lot of accounts of Near-Death Experiencers (NDE-ers) who described the expansiveness of what they experienced when they "crossed over," and how hard it was to come back to the reality of life on earth.

I felt like all the new things I was learning put flesh on the bones of the faith I was brought up with. These ideas were turning my religious platitudes into practical applications. For example:

Platitude: Angels exist. *Practical application*: In addition to my dedicated guardian angel, I can call on various types of angels to help me in any particular situation.

Platitude: Life is eternal. *Practical application*: Life is energy. Energy can neither be created nor destroyed. Life/energy continues to exist and we are all part of that, whether in our bodies or outside of them. Everything is part of an eternal web of connection.

Platitude: Heaven is a wonderful place. *Practical application*: There are infinite realms and possibilities to explore after we leave our bodies—adventures upon adventures in realms of light and love! All for the purpose of continual growth and expansion. (And we can begin to experience that even here in the physical.)

More Than a Single Decision...

During the summers, Luke loved to go to a Christian camp called IdRaHaJe in the foothills not far from Denver. We often thought he probably felt most at home there, with a bunch of campers his own age, overseen by a few caregivers, like the orphanage scenario where he spent the first two formative years of his life.

After Luke died, IdRaHaJe sent us a photo of Luke's signature in their "Book of Life" as a gesture of comfort. Luke's signature signified that he had made the personal decision to believe in Jesus and so he was guaranteed a spot in heaven.

I understand where the IdRaHaJe people were coming from. We shared the Christian belief that Jesus is our only way to God, and we have to believe that Jesus died for our sins in order to go to heaven (and not hell). We shared the belief that this is the most important decision you can make in your life, guaranteeing eternal bliss rather than eternal punishment.

However, receiving that news from IdRaHaJe that day did not comfort me. At best, it felt like another platitude; at worst, it almost felt like an insult. It felt like dry theology—like in the face of the unspeakable tragedy of the death of my son, we were concerned with checking boxes. How can a whole life be condensed into one question, one decision made? It seemed cheap, a demeaning and diminishing of all that was and is Luke. Surely he was more than just a tally mark in some heavenly ledger. Surely he made many more decisions, "good" and "bad," that had many effects on many people, including himself. His life was richer, deeper, more expansive, more impactful than that one decision to write his name in a book. Receiving a photo of Luke's signature did not seem to me to be an honoring of his life. It felt like a diminishing of it.

Trading My Bridge for a Train Track

That moment reminded me of my son J, when he was a kinder-gartener riding in the back of the van, praying to let Jesus into his heart because I had told him that's the key to not going to hell. And all the evangelism in Bible College and beyond: knocking on the doors of strangers or coming to the pivotal point in a community Bible study and asking people if they've made that crucial decision for Jesus to be their Savior. And when they did, it felt more like I had coerced them, that fear (of hell) was the motivator, rather than that a burden had been lifted or a truth had been discovered. If I had been honest, doing that never quite sat right with me. But it was what I believed, and what I had been taught to believe, and so I persisted.

I think it was Richard Rohr who first challenged me to think differently about the theology I was raised with. I remember being at a conference in which he was featured, several years before Luke died. There was a related art show presented in an adjoining room in the hotel, and I wandered through it between sessions. One particular piece caught my attention. It was simply a train track going through a field, presented in a kind of interactive way, so that the track opened up to the viewer. In other words, if a train came down that track, you as the viewer would be hit head on. Gazing at that painting, truth hit me in much the same way.

In Bible College I had been taught the "Bridge Illustration" as a tool for evangelism. We would draw two upside-down Ls as cliffs on opposite sides of a piece of paper. We as sinful people are on one side, God as the holy supreme being is on the other, and there is a huge chasm between us. Then we'd explain the story of Jesus' sacrifice for our sins and draw a cross across the chasm. Jesus' sacrifice makes it possible for us to walk across the gap of separation and access God. When we believe in Jesus, our relationship with God is restored. When I saw the train track coming toward me in that painting, I realized, "No, we're not separate from God, He's the very track we're running on! He's the foundation, the framework, the Something that holds it all together, on which our very lives depend. How can it be any other way?" God has never been separate; He's always been and will always be the Foundation. At that moment, that revelation brought tears to my eyes. It felt like a deep truth, like a relief, like a knowing I could trust-fall into.

Moving from Fear to Love

When Luke was in elementary school we started attending African-Caribbean Heritage Camp. The mission of Heritage Camps for Adoptive Families (HCAF) is to promote healthy adoptive, racial, and ethnic identities in transracial, transnational, and domestic adoptees. A large part of that is educating parents. I think it was at our first camp that we listened to a presentation by Bryan Post, author of *From Fear to Love: Parenting Difficult Adopted Children.*

Bryan explained many of the concepts that would later be solidified in me through TBRI. He was all about trauma-informed caregiving. He explained that our adopted children with difficult behaviors are not generally being willfully disobedient but are coping with dysregulated nervous systems as a result of the trauma(s) they've experienced. Their calming systems and brains have been hijacked; they live in survival mode. Their brains have to be rewired and recalibrated to a state of regulation. That happens through consistent, connected, calm caregiving which helps the child deeply integrate a feeling of safety into their brains and nervous systems. It requires a new, non-traditional way of parenting—one focused more on emotional connection than on reward/punishment/logic. It requires a commitment to changing behavior through love and connection rather than fear and punishment.

Changing my parenting paradigm was like trying to change the direction of a steam ship with a paddle boat rudder. My parenting ship had been cruising along just fine with how I had been parented and how we had parented our older three children. According to that paradigm, the more challenging the behaviors, the more we as parents needed to reinforce the boundaries and consistently apply the consequences/punishments. As I mentioned in the last section, that wasn't working with Luke. But his challenges were like a small rudder on a huge ship that had set sail a long time ago.

It occurs to me now that I was immersed in a parenting model based on fear, much like my Christian theology was based on fear. The idea of a judging, punishing God is not only in the Christianity I grew up with, but in our western culture as well. We love to punish the "bad" guy, bring swift justice to the wicked. I'm coming to believe that this is an old model. It's the way we survived in times of tribal warfare, when our amygdalas and our flight-or-fight brains ruled and guaranteed our continuing existence.

But doesn't being human mean we're more than our survival instincts? We're capable of creating, loving, caring for our neighbors, forgiving our enemies, negotiating and compromising, and living beyond black and white categories. We can think abstractly, come up with creative solutions, imagine something new. Our capacities as humans go far beyond the "let's destroy our enemies" mentality. And if we are so much more than that, how can the God who created us not be much, much, much, much, infinitely much more than that?

I wish I had parented Luke better: operated more out of love than fear. I wish I had made the emotional connection between us my priority at all times instead of reinforcing rules and consequences to no avail. But I was exhausted and running on autopilot most of the time, falling back again and again on the old fear-based model.

In spite of all the sub-messages about sin, judgment, and hell that I received throughout my Christian life, the overriding theme, in every church I've been a part of, has been that God is love. I've come to believe that love is a much more powerful force than fear. I don't believe in fear as a motivator anymore, in parenting or in religion. Using fear may work short-term but it's not a source of lasting change and it does damage to relationships. I no longer believe in the kind of Christianity that uses fear of hell to push people towards Jesus. I no longer believe in the systems of fear, whether in parenting or religion.

God is love. "There is no fear in love, but perfect love drives out fear, because fear expects punishment. The person who is afraid has not been made perfect in love" (1 John 4:18).

The Unforgivable Sin

Many Christians believe that taking one's own life may be the ultimate sin, may be the unforgivable sin, may guarantee that person's entrance into hell. Of course, I do not believe that. I may have wondered about that in the past, as a devoted Christian, but I definitely do not believe that today.

Luke ended his suicide note with, "to the people who judge me, rightfully so." I, for one, have never judged Luke for taking his own life. As I stated in my eulogy for Luke, ultimately, life was God's gift to Luke and ultimately, Luke could choose what to do with it. That is the gift (and sometimes the curse) of free will. In the end, Luke was in total control of his own life, probably for the first time in his life. He lived in a world of pain that none of us could fully grasp. At that moment in his life, this was the only way he could see out.

If I, as Luke's human, earthly mother, can understand his predicament and have mercy and compassion, how much more is God, Luke's Creator, my Creator, and the Creator of the universe to boot, capable of understanding, mercy, and compassion? Would He hold Himself to a set of rules and standards (suicide is an unforgiveable sin, therefore Luke must go to hell) over the pure love for what He has created? I refuse to believe in a God that has less compassion than I do. I refuse to believe in a God whose love is limited and constricted by self-imposed systems. (And actually I don't believe God has such systems—I believe they've been invented by men and imposed on God.)

How we talk about suicide reinforces that association with an "unforgivable sin." Referring to the act of suicide as "committing" suicide contributes to the idea of the immorality of suicide. The word "committed" puts suicide in the category of breaking the law, as if suicide is a crime. In fact, legally, in the USA and in most parts of the world, suicide is not a crime. However, it is still stigmatized as such, as our language reflects. And law enforcement is necessarily involved when someone takes their own life, to ensure no foul play, to ensure that no one else was responsible. We were not able to rush to the side of Luke when or after he died. The area was cordoned off with crime scene tape and we were told to stay back. His body was taken away by ambulance to the morgue and not released until the autopsy was completed.

The police investigative unit at the scene did have a victims' advocate who came and talked with us briefly. I remember she told me that being suicidal and struggling with mental health is like cancer: some people survive it and some don't. That's true, and that truth did provide some comfort. But if my son had had cancer, I could've been by his side at the time of his death, and his last thought would not have been about people judging him. No one talks about someone "committing" cancer. That would be ridiculous. No one asks for cancer, no one hopes and dreams for cancer, and dying of cancer is not against the law. The psychological struggle that leads to suicide is the same: no one asks for it, no one hopes and dreams for it, and suicide is not against the law. We need to change our language and stop the judgment. I say that Luke "died, or passed, by" suicide, just as we'd say someone died of cancer, or in a car accident, or of old age.

I'm not sure I ever believed in unforgivable sins, but I definitely do not believe in them now.

The Big, Beautiful Truth

I heard recently that "truth does not require belief." In other words, truth is truth, regardless of whether people believe it or not. We don't have to protect the truth—in fact, it protects us. It's a kind of law of the universe that "truth will prevail." We don't have to worry about letting go of what we know. In fact, sometimes we need to let go so that truth can find us.

Before Luke died, I was already on the path to thinking differently about my theology. But his death catapulted my launch into

134

a deeper and wider spirituality, one that embraces God as a wildly benevolent, merciful, continually creating Source. I'm still learning to trust a completely good God and to believe that our world can be, and is meant to be, a beautiful, nurturing place where we can experience continual expansion and creativity and love. I believe Luke is now back in a space where he knows and is experiencing that reality, and is urging me (and us) to remember it.

LESSON NINE

It's Not "Just" Your Imagination

We perceive what we believe.

—*theoretical physicist David Bohm*

"I have to see it to believe it" is a phrase we are very familiar with. It reflects the materialistic perspective we swim in in our western culture. If science can't measure or explain something, that thing is not real. If we can't experience it with our five physical senses, it doesn't exist. "I won't believe it until I see it."

What if there's a whole category of things we can't see unless we first believe in them? Or at least believe that they are possible? What if believing *precedes* perceiving?

Imagination as a Gateway to Truth

When we use our imaginations, daring to go beyond that which is commonly accepted as "real," we can discover truth. Galileo had to *imagine* that it was possible that the earth may not be the center of our solar system, before he could actually direct his studies in that direction and find that—surprise!—the sun is our center. The Wright brothers had to *imagine* that it was possible to create a machine that could fly, before they could invest all the time and money necessary to—voila!—be the first humans to experience flight. Martin Luther King Jr. had to *imagine* that it was possible for Americans to overcome the dynamics of slavery and create racial equity, before he could dedicate his life and even die for that cause, beginning an irreversible cascade of social change.

Galileo, the Wright brothers, and Martin Luther King (and I'm sure you can think of many others) had to use their imaginations to go beyond their current experience, beyond what was "real" and acceptable in their time, to demonstrate what was true. All of them were ridiculed and scorned and two even died for going against the status quo, for daring to prove the existence of an alternate reality. The basic rule is, if anything is outside of our "normal", mutually accepted experience, it's chalked up to our imagination and judged as "not real." You may be ridiculed for talking or even thinking about those things.

I recently heard someone say that if you can imagine it, it exists. There is nothing that we can think up that isn't already out there in some form, otherwise we wouldn't be able to imagine it. What a wonder-full world!

What does all this have to do with Luke and our story? Now that Luke's in spirit, my still-embodied spirit can see and communicate with him through my imagination. My rational mind, my ego, my intellect, can't get me there. I have to reach the world beyond my physical reality, beyond my five senses, beyond what the status quo may consider "real," through my imagination.

I was raised with prayer, which I did a LOT of in my life, as a Christian and a Christian missionary. Prayer was basically giving your list of requests to God, hoping that He would answer in alignment with your desires but trusting that if He didn't, it was for the penultimate good of all involved even if you couldn't always understand it. I never learned about meditation. Meditation does not involve any lists. It's kind of the opposite. It's about quieting the mind, going beyond the lists and worries, and connecting with something bigger, something truer, something beyond the status quo, beyond what's normally considered "real" in this life.

After Luke died, I learned more about meditation and how it can serve as a tool to connect with Spirit, and spirit. Step one is quieting the mind, which is not easy. Deep breaths, certain music/tones, smells, and having a relaxing environment can help. Many meditation teachers also suggest "clearing your chakras," which means getting rid of as much negative energy as you can (you can do a Google search to learn more). Then, basically, you use your imagination! You imagine yourself expanding out from this physical reality, out from your body, out from the room you're in, out into the universe... You imagine yourself going beyond what you know, beyond your experience, into the realm of spirit. Amazingly, spirit meets you there.

Connecting with Luke in spirit, whether during my own meditations or through healers who incorporate spirit-connection with other more traditional modalities (thank you to Crystal Derksen, Benny R Ferguson Jr., Peter DeBenedittis and *The Emotion Code*, Christine Bergstrom, Steve Burgess, and sound healings with Candace Blair and Andrea Courey), has been a big part of my healing journey (and the writing of this book). Some may say these encounters are "just my imagination" and I'm a bit coo-coo. I say: I'm so thankful for my imagination, that I have the possibility and ability to expand beyond what I'm experiencing in my physical reality and connect with my son (and so much else in the world of spirit)!

Some time ago I watched a panel of experts being interviewed at the International Association of Near-Death Experiencers (IANDS) conference. Someone asked how you can discern between psychosis (craziness) and "realness" when it comes to people's experiences with, let's say, what's beyond. The answer one of the experts gave was that if the person's experiences help them to function better in life, to lead more loving, fuller lives, to heal, then those experiences are "real." If, by contrast, those experiences lead the person to more fear and dysfunction in their lives, that's psychosis. That made a lot of sense to me. I feel more sane, more whole now, connecting to spirit through meditation and imagination, than I did in all the years I adhered strictly to the accepted, status-quo Christian beliefs and practices. It is unlikely I would've discovered this world, this expanded reality, if Luke had not led me there. Him leaving his physical body gave me the motivation to imagine the possibilities.

Permission

Sometimes we can be scared of our imaginations. Probably because they lead us into the unknown, into things we've never experienced before, and that feels threatening. Rules and predictability make us feel safe.

A couple of years before this writing, I volunteered for a semester with AmeriCorps at Montessori del Mundo elementary school in their Social-Emotional Learning department. During my orientation I was observing a preschool class and had the privilege of sitting in a child-sized chair beside two 4-year-old girls who were busy coloring animal printouts. They had models to follow, with coloring that matched what they would see in the "real" world. The one girl, J, was coloring a turtle and asked her classmate, M, to borrow a pink pencil crayon so she could color her turtle's tail pink. M refused because turtles have brown tails, not pink ones! I encouraged J to find a pink pencil crayon somewhere else, which she did, and continued happily coloring. Meanwhile M became increasingly angry because J wasn't following the rules and the example of the brown-tailed turtle. M sat with her arms tightly crossed, a mad frown on her face, and refused to color her own horse.

After an appropriate time of festering, M finally decided to get coloring. To my surprise, she produced a multi-colored horse! It was a beautiful patchwork of many different colors—wonderful! I praised her creativity and she smiled proudly, a complete turn-around from her earlier frustration.

Opening our minds to imagination and possibilities beyond reality as we know it can feel scary, threatening, and sometimes even make us angry. We may want to shout, "Hey! That person's not following the rules!" It's hard to let go of what's familiar, of the boundaries that make us feel safe. Sometimes we just need one person's permission, through their example, to explore beyond the boundaries of what we know. And then we find that there's a lot of joy to be had when we allow our imaginations, our creativity, to guide us into what exists beyond…

LESSON TEN

Be the Light You Are

You are the light of the world.

—*Jesus, Matthew 5:14*

The light shines in the darkness and the darkness has not overcome it.

—*John 1:5*

We are stars with skin. The light we are seeking is always within.

—*Rumi*

Pineapple Paradigm

I've cut a lot of pineapples in my life. It's kind of tricky to do, maneuvering through and around the tough, prickly skin as well as the fibrous, stiff inner core. I probably learned how to cut a pineapple the year we lived in Costa Rica, the country responsible for producing the majority of pineapples in the world. The prize inside—that sweet, juicy, golden-yellow "mesocarp" as they call it—was well worth the effort.

Maybe we can look at life like a pineapple. First, we have the tough, fibrous inner *core* that runs vertically through the fruit. I've learned that, technically, a pineapple is a mass of individual berries fused to that central stalk. So the core or stalk is the center of the fruit, not only geographically but also developmentally. Everything grows out from the core. Interestingly, the core of the pineapple is usually a little lighter in color (a lighter yellow) than the fleshy part that we eat.

You might say the core is the essence of the pineapple—it's what's left at the center when you strip everything else away. People debate about what is at the core of us as humans, and at the core of our universe. Are we, is our universe, essentially good or evil, light or dark? What is left when everything is stripped away? I'd like to suggest Light. Light is left. Light is the core. Light is the thing that everything eventually implodes into. It is the essence of what's going on here. Ultimately, everything returns to light because at the core, everything is light. I suppose I've always believed this, in one form or another, but through Luke's life and death, I feel like I'm now experiencing it. I'm coming to *know* that there is light beyond the darkness. That the ultimate reality is light.

Back to the pineapple… surrounding the core is the fleshy part: that sweet, juicy *mesocarp* that pineapple lovers long to sink their teeth into. It's the "meat" of the pineapple, the part we want to dig into and taste, to suck all the goodness out of. The mesocarp in a fresh, ripe pineapple is usually a deep golden yellow, rich and vibrant. Cutting a pineapple is a messy job—the juice from the mesocarp runs down the knife and onto the cutting board and beyond. And the juice is acidic. If you happen to have an open cut or sore that the juice runs into, you'll know it.

The light within us, and within the universe, naturally expands. It does so through experience, through rubbing up against things that are not light, or not yet light. We can think of the pineapple mesocarp as symbolic of our life experiences. What we experience is the "meat" of our lives, the fleshy part that we can sink our teeth into. Our experiences are both sweet and biting, pleasurable and stinging; through them we taste the multi-faceted deliciousness of our lives. We grow and expand through what we experience, becoming a deeper and more vibrant version of ourselves—the light of our cores filling with more subtle hues and tones, becoming more beautiful, more tactile, more whole.

Finally, there's the *skin* of the pineapple—that tough, spiky protective layer surrounding everything. What is our skin, the thing containing all our light and all our experience? Love. I like to think of love as containing it all. Love is that tenacious, enduring, protective force that encompasses everything. Love honors the processes our experiences take us through. It functions like the skin of the pineapple, ensuring that no drop of the sweet, stinging juice of our experiences leaks out unused or wasted. Love is holding us and everything together.

You have to be patient with pineapples. It takes three years for a pineapple plant to produce its first fruit, and then a full year to produce each single fruit after that. The good news is that a pineapple plant can survive up to 50 years! It takes time to accept and adopt the pineapple paradigm as a habitual way of thinking. Sometimes it does not feel like we are light, like our experiences are delicious, and like love is holding everything together. However, over time, and ultimately, I believe we will all experience this to be true.

The Story of the Epitaph: Be the Light You Are

D and I had a hard time coming up with an epitaph for Luke's memorial boulder. How do you condense a whole life, and all the experiences we had with Luke, into just a few words? And certainly we didn't want to resort to some trite phrase of comfort like "Rest in peace" or "He's with Jesus now." For the record, we did believe Luke was and is at rest with Jesus. Actually, maybe it's *because* we believed those things that we didn't feel the necessity to etch the words into a rock for posterity. We didn't feel the need to make that kind of statement.

I began to ask Luke, in meditation, what he would want etched on his boulder, and tried to listen for a response or impression.

On January 21, 2023, I had a session with Crystal Derksen, one of several I was privileged to have with her. Crystal helped me integrate the trauma I experienced with Luke's passing through a therapeutic technique called EFT/"tapping." She wove that technique beautifully with her ability to connect with spirit, especially with Jesus (Crystal is a Christian) and also with Luke.

During this particular session Crystal "saw" both Jesus and Luke with us. She said, "Luke is seeing the light inside himself! He keeps pointing to it."

That image brought tears to my eyes. It seemed Luke could never see the light in himself while embodied on this earth. I think he could rarely see anything but darkness. There is a Bible verse, in the book of Romans, that says something like, "The things I want to do, I don't do, and the things I don't want to do, those are the things I do. What a wretched man I am!" Luke lived with a constant internal struggle. He would show his light—his helpfulness, his compassion, his skills and talents—in bright and temporary flashes. But it was like it was too much for him to fully claim those things about himself, to live out of his goodness. He would revert back to what he fundamentally believed about himself: that he was no good, a failure, something that needed fixing. And then he would live and behave out of those dark beliefs.

Even now it brings me to tears to think about Luke proudly acknowledging the light inside himself. Crystal went on to relate that Luke was saying: "Mom, this is my new perception, this is who I am. I know who I am now. Mom, you've got to see the light inside of *you*." Luke said that he was growing in his true identity and wanted me to as well. He gave me homework, to repeat the mantras: "I am whole. I am light. Everything is whole." He finished with, "Mom, you're not making this up. This is real!"

A couple of days later I started receiving what would become a recurring vision of myself and Luke, dressed like a queen and prince, light like the sun shining out of our chests. We are standing on the edge of a beautiful cliff, looking towards a city far off in the distance. The feeling as we stand there is one of commissioning, like we are getting ready to do something together for the good of the people in that city. I don't fully know what the vision means but I do know how it makes me feel: comforted, hopeful, inspired.

A few days after receiving that vision, I received the phrase "The Luke Project." At the time I didn't know what The Luke Project would be, but I took note of it.

February 1, 2023 (two years ago to the day, as I write this) was my first day as an AmeriCorps volunteer at Montessori del Mundo elementary school. I was working with the Social-Emotional Learning (SEL) department. Every department had a name, and SEL's was Las Estrellas—the stars! I was literally part of the star department. A reinforcement, in the physical, of the reality I was learning in the non-physical: We are light. Sometimes the kids would even call my supervisor, the head of the department, "Ms. Estrella" instead of her name. To top it off, the next morning I stood beside "Ms. Estrella" to welcome the kids into school. One preschooler made it a particular point to show me her star necklace, which was big and green and contained a solution with which to blow bubbles. (Green is typically associated with our heart chakra, from which the light of our love shines.)

At that time I also happened to be reading the book *Quarks of Light* with a dear friend. We were finishing up the book that first week of February and the author, Rob Gentile, concludes with his realization (from his near-death experience) that we are all points,

151

or quarks, of light. I also happened to read that month, in *We're Not Dead, Just Different*, that babies who are aborted appear as twinkling lights behind the shoulders of their moms. In an online meditation I happened to do with Suzanne Giesemann, I was encouraged to "develop the light within me." Messages of light were appearing everywhere.

For Luke's birthday that year (2/23/23) we gifted him a star named after him, in the Orion constellation, to honor his light. Some believe there is a galactic history that we are rarely taught. In that history, Orion is known as the warring constellation, where races fought for domination. It seemed fitting to place Luke's star there, to symbolize the warring that went on inside his own psyche, within our family, and in the prejudiced society in which he struggled to find his place. For our daughter, L, Orion connected to Frank Ocean's song "Orion (Oh, Ryan)." Ocean dedicated that song to his younger brother, encouraging him not to waste his young years. It conveys the love and protection of an older sibling, as L was to Luke.

Around this same time, one night as I was falling asleep, I received the phrase, "Be the Light You Are." Ah!—that would be Luke's epitaph, to honor the light in him and in us all.

Falling Stars

Luke fell to his death, his own choice, his own method.

What once made me shudder to my core and cry out—that image of him falling—now seems like more.

It seems like a message.

What if Luke went out the way he came in, the way we all do?

Maybe, like him, we're all falling stars making our way down to earth to shine what light we can.

Maybe "the dust we came from and to which we shall return" is actually stardust.

Maybe the darkness we find ourselves in is only the necessary backdrop for our lights to appear even brighter.

Maybe this whole experience: light, dark, life, death, joy, pain—maybe it's all a gift we've given ourselves.

When we open it fully, when we live through it all as authentically as we can, our lights grow brighter, deeper, wider, more beautiful.

We see you, Luke, shining like you were meant to all along. Help us do the same.

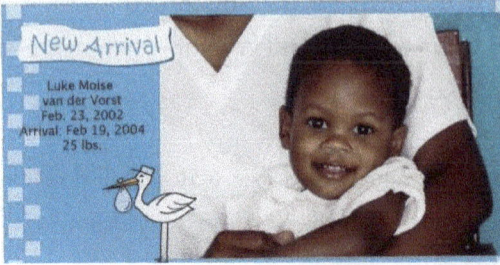

New Arrival

Luke Moise
van der Vorst
Feb. 23, 2002
Arrival: Feb 19, 2004
25 lbs.

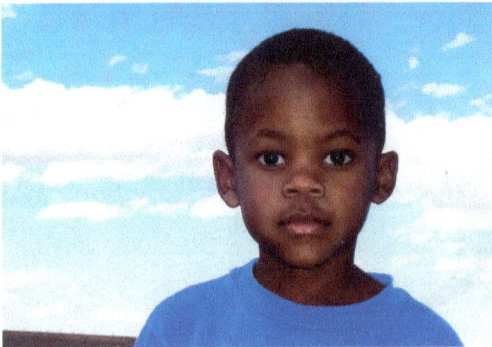

Thank you for investing your time and energy in reading this book! If you would like to reach out to me for any reason you can contact me at TheLukeProject23@gmail.com. Let's walk this road together.

www.ingramcontent.com/pod-product-compliance
Lightning Source LLC
Chambersburg PA
CBHW071440090426
42737CB00011B/1735